Submarines
In Color

Bill Gunston

Submarines
In Color

Illustrated by

John W. Wood
B. Hiley
J. Pelling
E. Bruce

ARCO PUBLISHING COMPANY, INC
New York

Published 1977 by Arco Publishing Company, Inc.
219 Park Avenue South, New York, N.Y. 10003

Printed in Great Britain

Library of Congress Cataloging in Publication Data

Gunston, Bill.
  Submarines in color.

  Includes index.
  1. Submarine boats—History. I. Title.
VM365.G78   359.8'3   76-27851
ISBN 0-668-04107-2
ISBN 0-668-04255 pbk.

CONTENTS

The author is especially grateful to Cdr P. R. Compton-Hall, M.B.E., R.N., Rtd, Curator, Submarine Museum, H.M.S. Dolphin, Gosport, Hants, U.K., for reading the script of this book and for his helpful advice and criticisms.

INTRODUCTION

The seas are a hostile place. Though an increasing proportion of the world's population are learning to skin-dive, and to feel at home within the marine environment, this is still only playing around the edges. Even the Continental Shelf around most of the land masses poses underwater problems that technology cannot yet completely solve, while the deep oceans have been rightly called the last great unexplored part of our planet. Their immensity is awesome—the Pacific Ocean alone is much bigger in surface area than all the land on Earth—and the pressures in their depths are incapable of being imagined.

Into this challenging environment man must advance by small steps. An early Egyptian wall painting shows duck hunters walking on the river bed, breathing (schnorkelling?) through reeds at least 4,000 years ago. The diving bell, in which air is trapped beneath a heavy bell-shaped container, was certainly familiar at the time of Aristotle in 330 B.C. From there it is not a great mental leap to the submarine, capable of locomotion; yet though Da Vinci (c.1500) and British naval officer William Bourne (1578) described and sketched suggestions, there is no evidence that anybody built one until the seventeenth century. Even then it took a long time for improving technology to make possible a submarine that could be described as practical. Until a mere century ago no submarine could be described as reliable, useful or even safe.

This question of 'use' is central to what is meant by the word 'submarine'. Though it is still a matter for debate, the word has for a century been taken to mean a vessel of warlike purpose; it is described as such in most dictionaries. This reflects the sad fact that virtually every submarine built between 1750 and 1950 had as its primary purpose the destruction of other ships. Only in the past quarter century have numerous civil submarines been built, for underwater exploration, research, salvage, seabed construction projects, rescue, and other purposes which need not be warlike at all. These civil craft are generally called submersibles, and are described in the companion volume *The Seas and Oceans in Colour*.

Almost all the first submarines—those built in the century from 1775—had as their objective the destruction of ships of a powerful enemy fleet, as a way of raising a hurtful naval blockade. For this task the performance objectives, in terms of speed and range, did not have to be challenging. The submarine, by its very nature, is both hidden by the sea and also largely protected by it against attack by gunfire. In its early days it was a creature not of speed but of stealth. Walking pace was amply fast enough; it was much more important that its progress should be silent than swift. As for range, a mile or two was usually more than enough—until the blockading fleet heard rumours of submarines being built, or were actually attacked on dark nights, when they would stand off at what seemed a prudent distance. In general, the limiting factor in submarine performance was the air supply. With all hatches closed, the oxygen was progressively used up and the crew could become drowsy and lethargic. This was later found to be potentially lethal, just as is oxygen deficiency at high altitudes, in dulling the senses and inhibiting remedial action.

By 1875 it was possible to mate the submarine with the self-propelled torpedo and produce a vastly different kind of vessel. Instead of merely raising a blockade, the submarine could in theory now go out and sink ships in the open ocean. Though it became apparent only very slowly, and was not fully appreciated until a few days after the outbreak of World War 1, the lowly submarine was capable of revolutionizing naval warfare. Even more than this, it was capable of severing sea trade links, and bringing any nation that depended on overseas supplies to its knees.

All this was very much contrary to what were rather nicely called 'the rules of war'. Warfare was a game for gentlemen, and nothing so infuriated the professional soldier or sailor as the emergence of a new method of waging war that did not fit the rules. An improved hand-gun or artillery piece was acceptable, because it was new only in degree; a submarine was quite new in concept, and therefore wholly unacceptable. The French under Napoleon told one inventor his submarine was 'fit only for Algerians and pirates'. A famous British admiral called the submarine 'damned un-English', and another threatened that if he ever caught a submarine crew he would hang them from the yardarm! Perhaps more logical was the opinion of Admiral St Vincent that the submarine offered 'a mode of war which they who commanded the seas did not want, and which, if successful, would deprive them of it'. In World War 1 the German U-boats were constantly either kept on a tight rein and used in a restrictive way, or else allowed to sink merchant ships and cause shrieks of horror that damaged German prestige and, ultimately, caused the United States to enter the war on the side of the Allies. The same thing was repeated in the early days of World War 2, when Hitler hoped to avoid real conflict with Britain and France and was anxious not to inflame public opinion in those countries.

By 1945 several revolutions had taken place. Once and for all the notion that there are 'rules of war' had been recognised as not supportable by the facts. No longer was there any distinction between combatants and non-combatants. Though individuals, including submarine captains of all nations, might sometimes act in what could be described as unnecessarily humane ways, it was henceforth taken for granted that in wartime enemy ships of any kind are liable to be sunk by submarines, probably without warning. A second revolution was the swift growth of effective ways of finding, chasing and destroying submerged submarines. Conversely, a third revolution was the dramatic improvement in the submerged speed of submarines which became possible at the end of World War 2.

At first this improved performance was due to new hull forms, fatter than the traditional shape but better streamlined, and to improved propulsion machinery of much greater power. But a more fundamental revolution in underwater performance stemmed after World War 2 from the harnessing of nuclear energy. Previously submarines had been strictly limited in the actual quantity of propulsive energy they could carry. If their submerged speed was no more than 10 knots (18 km/hr) they could travel from tens to hundreds of miles submerged. With improved methods of ASW (anti-submarine warfare) such a speed was inadequate; yet faster travel underwater consumed propulsive energy at a prodigious rate, because the drag (resistance to motion) increases roughly as the cube of the speed. Thus, if a submarine needs 1,000 h.p. (746 kW) to run submerged at 10 knots, it will need at least 8,000 h.p. to run at 20. Suddenly, with nuclear power, there was no more problem. It multiplied the quantity of stored energy by as many times as the designer wished.

Whereas previous submarines had been—of necessity—surface vessels which could temporarily submerge, the nuclear submarine was a true submarine. The depth of the ocean is its natural habitat. It does not only travel many times further underwater but it also travels much faster. Not merely slightly faster but so much faster that the hostile surface vessel is outdistanced and the ASW aircraft is hard put to keep track of the racing monster of the depths. In the space of a few years in the early 1950s the nuclear submarine did as much to enhance the lethality of that species of weapon as the jet engine did for the combat aircraft.

Something else happened in the 1950s that brought about the second, and possibly final, revolution in the capability and purpose of the submarine. Since the early 1920s submarines had from time to time been equipped to carry and operate small aircraft. These were used mainly for reconnaissance, but the Japanese attempted to use more powerful aircraft which could have carried bombs, thus introducing the concept of sudden aerial attack from a long-range mobile base which could not be destroyed or even discovered in advance. By the late 1950s submarines were carrying jet-propelled guided missiles armed with nuclear warheads. The final development was to mate the submarine with the ballistic missile. After studying large and relatively clumsy liquid-propellant missiles, specially designed solid-fuel ballistic missiles were made in the USA and Soviet Union for submarine deployment, so compact that a single vessel could carry sixteen. Moreover, all sixteen could be fired while the submarine was hidden in the depths of the sea. Thus the submarine became a strategic weapon, a destroyer of distant cities and nations, and the primary carrier of the ultimate nuclear deterrent.

It followed that there was a vast increase in research funding to combat the submarine. The work began at the level of pure research into the ocean itself. What are the properties of sea-water, both in the test tube and in the vast ocean depths? How are sound waves and various kinds of electromagnetic wave propagated, attenuated and refracted? How can

9

such waves best be reflected from a submarine hull? Can one 'see' in the depth of the ocean, in the region of eternal darkness where steel hulls must resist pressures of about a ton on every square inch? Most frightening of all, how can submarines be prevented from ever sinking beyond their design depth until even the strongest hull is crushed like matchwood, as happened to an American submarine in 1963?

Today, billions of dollars and roubles (and a few pounds and francs) later, man has a much better understanding of the physics of the oceans. The knowledge has helped both submariners and those who seek to kill them. It has also enabled man to make much better use of the oceans, which contain a volume of water fifteen times larger than the total volume of all the land above sea level, and which must one day be recognised as our greatest storehouse of many raw materials. We should not be too surprised that, so far, most of the money spent on finding out about the oceans has been voted in order to improve man's ability to wage war within them.

DEVELOPMENT OF SUBMARINE TECHNOLOGY

Anti-submarine measures shown in italics.

Phase I: pre-1775

In this period the construction of a working submarine was an end in itself. Most recorded examples were built for fun, or as experiments, and were not weapons.

Technology available for submarine structures included hardwoods, leather and other animal skins, tar and established caulking methods, brass and copper straps and pins, and cordage. Technology available for propulsion included the sail, and muscle-power applied to oars, paddlewheels and screw propellers. *Anti-submarine technology included guns, nets and crude submarine mines.*

Phase II: 1775–1875

This was the century in which the submarine matured as a practical weapon. Nearly all those built were intended to travel only a short distance from their home port in order to sink a blockading enemy vessel.

1777 Bushnell invented crude submarine torpedo.

1780 From about this time shipwrights became skilled in the use of iron both for hull framing and, in the nineteenth century, for plating. In parallel came the progressive development of the steam boiler and various kinds of reciprocating steam engine.

1838 First surface vessel driven by crude electric motor. Electric storage batteries also progressively improved and refined from this period.

1860 Start of development of modern high-strength structural steels.

1865 Swift growth in development of internal-combustion engines, compressed-air motors and other mechanical power sources.

1869 Whitehead's first modern self-propelled torpedo, with gyro/pendulum stabilization. (Later the torpedo was also to become an *anti-submarine weapon.*)

1870 Earliest robust optical periscope.

Phase III: 1875–1960

This was the period in which the submarine emerged as a free-ranging weapon, capable of destroying all kinds of warships (including other submarines) and merchant vessels, and of exerting a major influence on naval warfare.

1880 First proper understanding of underwater stability and control. *Surface warships constructed for deliberate ramming of enemy vessels, including submarines.*

1890 Perfection of first methods of dual surface/submerged systems of propulsion.

1895 Refined hull designs, with the pressure hull surrounded by water ballast tanks encased in a ship-like outer hull.

1898 Long-endurance underwater propulsion with electric batteries rechargeable whilst at sea.

1906 Submarine diesel engines. Refined retractable periscopes of high optical quality.

1915 *Frantic development of stick bomb and thrower depth charge, depth-charge thrower (to give a controlled pattern) and underwater hydrophone.*

1916 Reconnaissance aircraft carried by submarine.

1917 *Convoy system for merchant shipping.*

1919 Submarine with heavy (12 in.) gun.

1925 *Accelerating research with Asdic by Anti-Submarine Devices Investigation Committee.*

1927 Submarine with hangar and crane for reconnaissance seaplane.

1930 From about this time, development of techniques of skin diving, leading to midget submarines and 'human torpedoes'.

1938 Schnorkel, allowing air-breathing (i.e., diesel) engines to run when submerged (Royal Netherlands Navy).

1940 *Rapid improvement of Asdic and ASW radar.*

1941 First experimental (land) nuclear reactor. Wolf-pack technique. *Anti-submarine mortar with fast-falling bomb.*

1942 *Hunter and killer aircraft.*

1943 Rotor kite towed by submarine to extend visual horizon. *Swift development of experimental sonobuoys.*

1944 Effective homing torpedoes. Greater electrical power and new chemical fuel enables submarines to run much faster underwater.

1948 Fat, streamlined 'spindle' hull form and streamlined sail allows yet higher underwater speed.

1955 *New ASW methods include helicopters, MAD equipment, diesel exhaust sniffer and the first guided long-range AS missiles.*

1956 Nuclear propulsion provides almost limitless installed energy for propulsion and life-support underwater, giving great submerged range and endurance at much higher speed. Design begun on first SLBM systems using Polaris and 'Sark' missiles.

Phase IV: since 1960

Today the submarine is no longer just a naval weapon but the main carrier of the strategic nuclear deterrent which can be employed over intercontinental ranges against enemy heartlands. (Though not the concern of this book, the modern scene also reflects vastly increased underwater activity of all kinds for numerous civil and military purposes, which may extend the ability of military submarines to dive much deeper.)

1960 Commissioning of first SSBN strategic-missile vessel.

1965 Swift progress in making submerged submarines acoustically quieter. *Conversely, steady progress in range and accuracy of underwater detection systems.*

1972 Rapid-reacting anti-aircraft guided missile system deployed aboard otherwise unmodified submarines.

THE COLOUR PLATES

Relevant textual matter may be referred to by comparison of the colour plate page number with the same number set in line with bold text headings.

De Son, 1653 These illustrations are based on the best contemporary drawings made at Rotterdam during construction of the wildly 'oversold' military submarine conceived by the Frenchman De Son. The blades on the paddle-wheel were apparently arranged by linkages always to lie vertical, but most recent observers have concluded that the scheme would not have worked. The crude rudder was intended to operate in the efflux behind the paddles.

18

Bushnell's Turtle, 1776 The first submarine known to have been used against an enemy.

A ventilator pipes; **B** auger; **C** vertical propeller; **D** horizontal propeller; **E** pump; **F** flooding valve; **G** ballast tank; **H** pump inlet; **J** permanent water ballast; **K** detachable lead keel; **L** seat and 'anti-pressure plank'; **M** auxiliary ballast pump inlet; **N** auxiliary pump; **O** rudder; **P** detonator; **Q** explosive charge (150 lb); **R** wooden keg; **S** attachment rope.

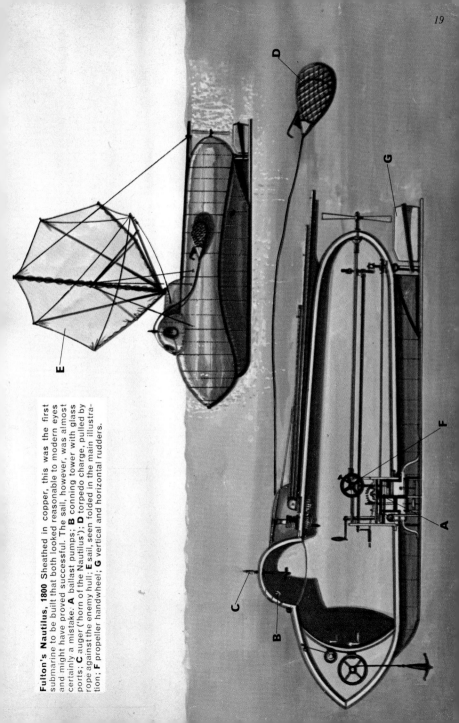

Fulton's Nautilus, 1800 Sheathed in copper, this was the first submarine to be built that looked reasonable to modern eyes and might have proved successful. The sail, however, was almost certainly a mistake. The sail, however, was almost certainly a mistake. **A** ballast pumps; **B** conning tower with glass ports; **C** auger ('horn of the Nautilus'); **D** torpedo charge, pulled by rope against the enemy hull; **E** sail, seen folded in the main illustration; **F** propeller handwheel; **G** vertical and horizontal rudders.

Bauer's Brandtaucher, 1850 Driven along by a screw geared-up from two treadmills, this military craft – also called Plongeur-Marin – appears to have been surprisingly well thought-out, especially in view of the apparent absence of any previous engineering or marine experience by its designer (an artillery corporal). Unlike the final design of Robert Fulton, which would have needed a crew of ninety, Bauer's design was operated by three men, each of whom had clearly assigned duties. The explosive charge (not shown) was to have been attached to the enemy hull by the commander, in the conning tower, using a pair of long rubber gloves sealed to two holes in the top of the tower. This is the earliest submarine of which photographs exist.

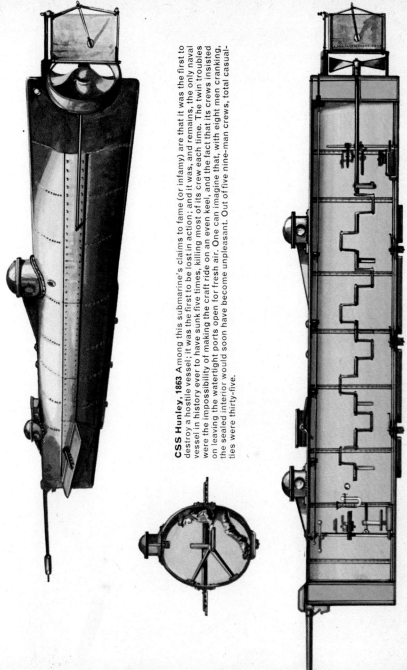

CSS Hunley, 1863 Among this submarine's claims to fame (or infamy) are that it was the first to destroy a hostile vessel; it was the first to be lost in action; and it was, and remains, the only naval vessel in history ever to have sunk five times, killing most of its crew each time. The twin troubles were the impossibility of making the craft ride on an even keel, and the fact that its crews insisted on leaving the watertight ports open for fresh air. One can imagine that, with eight men cranking, the sealed interior would soon have become unpleasant. Out of five nine-man crews, total casualties were thirty-five.

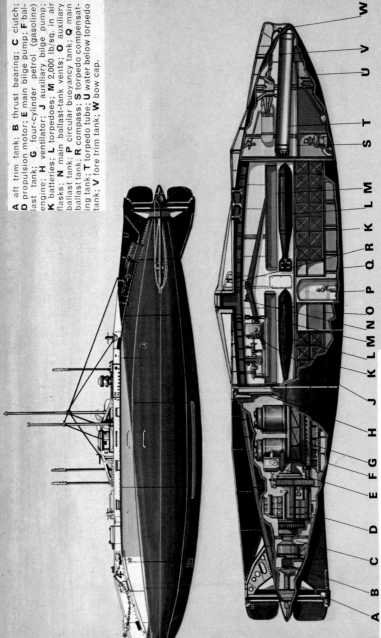

A aft trim tank; B thrust bearing; C clutch; D propulsion motor; E main bilge pump; F ballast tank; G four-cylinder petrol (gasoline) engine; H ventilator; J auxiliary bilge pump; K batteries; L torpedoes; M 2,000 lb/sq. in air flasks; N main ballast-tank vents; O auxiliary ballast tank; P circular buoyancy tank; Q main ballast tank; R compass; S torpedo compensating tank; T torpedo tube; U water below torpedo tank; V fore trim tank; W bow cap.

USS Holland, 1898 Widely regarded as the pioneer of the modern submarine, this outstanding design was possible only because of John P. Holland's long previous experience with less successful craft.

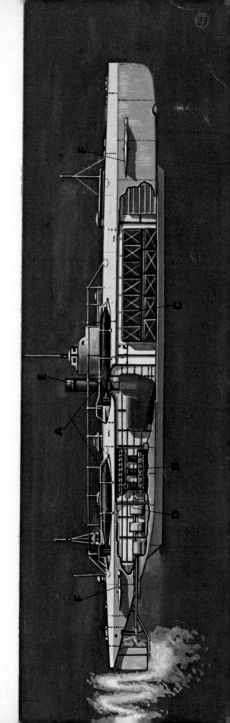

Laubeuf's Narval, 1899 In some ways even superior to the Holland designs, Narval looked on the surface like a contemporary steamdriven torpedo boat, and in fact used steam propulsion on the surface. This gave good speed, but prohibited rapid diving and made the interior stifling underwater. **A** externally carried torpedoes (four); **B** triple-expansion surface engine; **C** batteries; **D** electric motor; **E** funnel; **F** fore and aft planes.

24

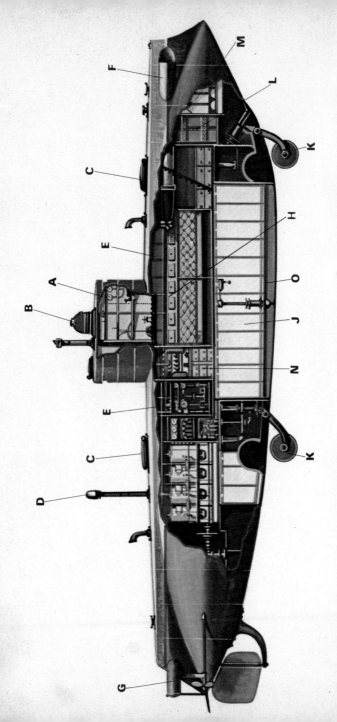

Lake's Protector, 1902 Simon Lakes' Argonaut can claim to have been the first submarine ever to make an ocean voyage, because in 1898 it travelled under its own power through November storms from Norfolk, Virginia, to New York – a remarkable feat. From it Lake developed this military craft, several of which were sold to Russia in 1906. **A** bronze conning tower; **B** sighting hood; **C** hatches; **D** exhaust; **E** petrol fuel; **F** two bow tubes; **G** stern tube; **H** crew space; **J** batteries; **K** retracting wheels; **L** airlock; **M** diving compartment giving access to sea; **N** galley; **O** drop keel.

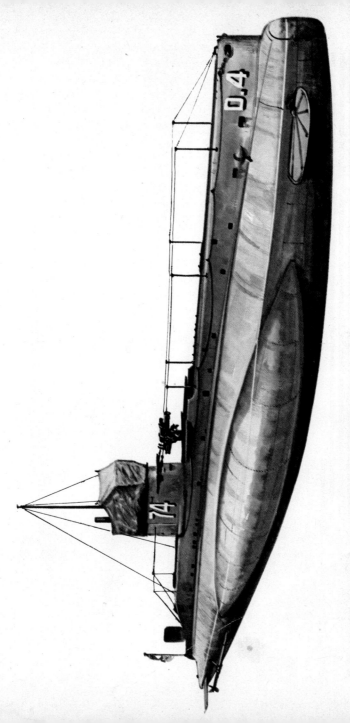

British D-class, 1910 These excellent vessels were designed on the basis of unrivalled experience of exacting submarine operation with the Holland-derived A, B and C. The D was much bigger, double-hulled like the French submarines of the time, and powered by some of the first marine diesel engines. Sea-keeping was markedly better than in the earlier boats, and D-class vessels served throughout World War II. They were probably the first submarines capable of safe ocean navigation.

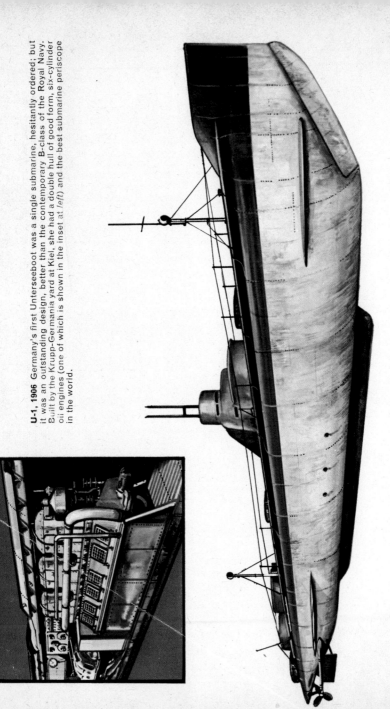

U-1, 1906 Germany's first Unterseeboot was a single submarine, hesitantly ordered; but it was an outstanding design, better than the contemporary B-class of the Royal Navy. Built by the Krupp-Germania yard at Kiel, she had a double hull of good form, six-cylinder oil engines (one of which is shown in the inset at *left*) and the best submarine periscope in the world.

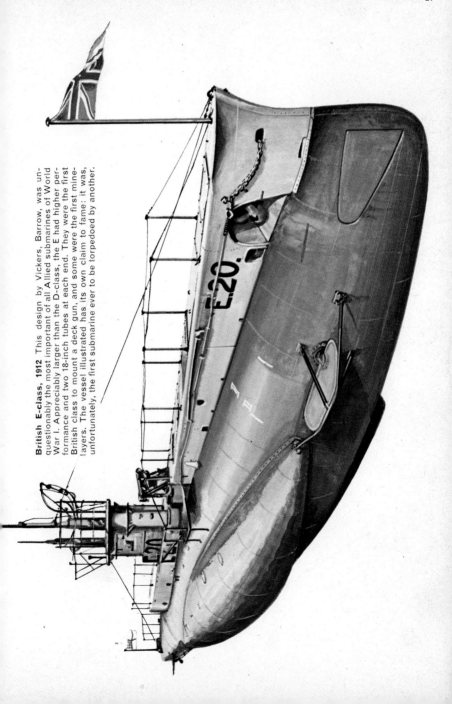

British E-class, 1912 This design by Vickers, Barrow, was unquestionably the most important of all Allied submarines of World War I. Appreciably larger than the D-class, the E had higher performance and two 18-inch tubes at each end. They were the first British class to mount a deck gun, and some were the first minelayers. The vessel illustrated has its own claim to fame: it was, unfortunately, the first submarine ever to be torpedoed by another.

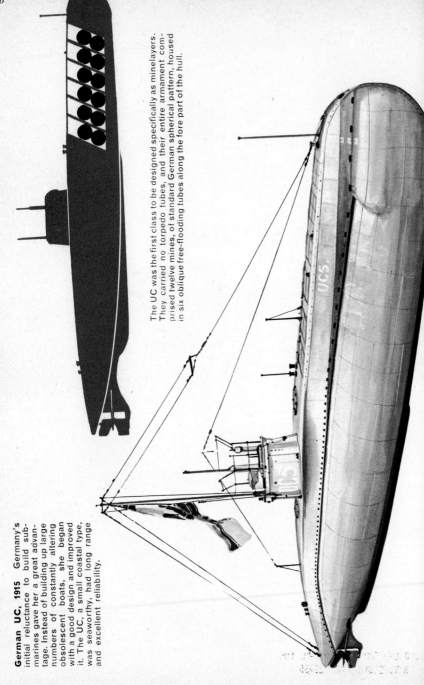

German UC, 1915 Germany's initial reluctance to build submarines gave her a great advantage. Instead of building up large numbers of constantly altering obsolescent boats, she began with a good design and improved it. The UC, a small coastal type, was seaworthy, had long range and excellent reliability.

The UC was the first class to be designed specifically as minelayers. They carried no torpedo tubes, and their entire armament comprised twelve mines, of standard German spherical pattern, housed in six oblique free-flooding tubes along the fore part of the hull.

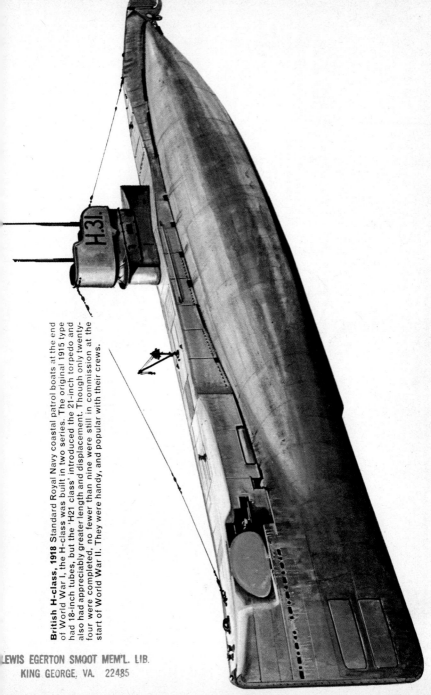

British H-class, 1918 Standard Royal Navy coastal patrol boats at the end of World War I, the H-class was built in two series. The original 1915 type had 18-inch tubes, but the 'H21 class' introduced the 21-inch torpedo and also had appreciably greater length and displacement. Though only twenty-four were completed, no fewer than nine were still in commission at the start of World War II. They were handy, and popular with their crews.

British K-class, 1916-23 The Admiralty retained an incessant and insatiable wish to build submarines fast enough to keep up with the surface fleet. Such speed could not be obtained with diesels – the triple-screw J-class proved this – so in the K-class steam turbines were fitted. They were extremely large boats and posed severe difficulties.

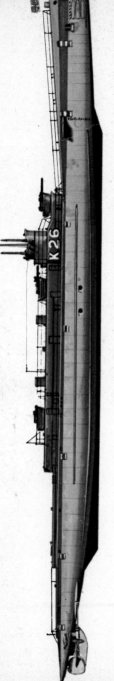

K26, 1923 This latecomer was a considerably different boat with greater length, modified hull, redesigned superstructure and armament of ten 21-inch tubes and three 4-inch guns. In view of the impossibility of making a furnace boiler submarine that could dive fast, and not get too hot inside the K-class were surprisingly successful.

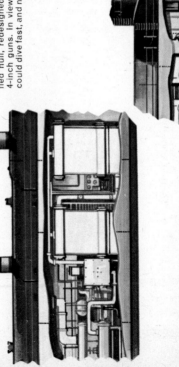

K9 details The three insets show portions of the front, middle and rear of one of the original series of K-class Fleet Submarines used in World War I. Of especial interest are the two large water-tube boilers, each with its own smoke stack.

British X-1, 1925 Launched in 1923, X-1 was a mystery ship, built and fitted out in the greatest secrecy. All the public knew was that she was to be 'an underwater cruiser'. She proved on her trials in 1925 not to have quite the 30-knot speed and ten big guns that some had predicted, but her capabilities were stunning nevertheless. Though she still stemmed from the ridiculous wish to keep up with the surface fleet, she did at least use diesels, and could not only dive far faster than a K-boat but also set records for deep diving and long range. Unfortunately her powerful diesel engines were unreliable, and for this reason she was stricken in 1936.

32

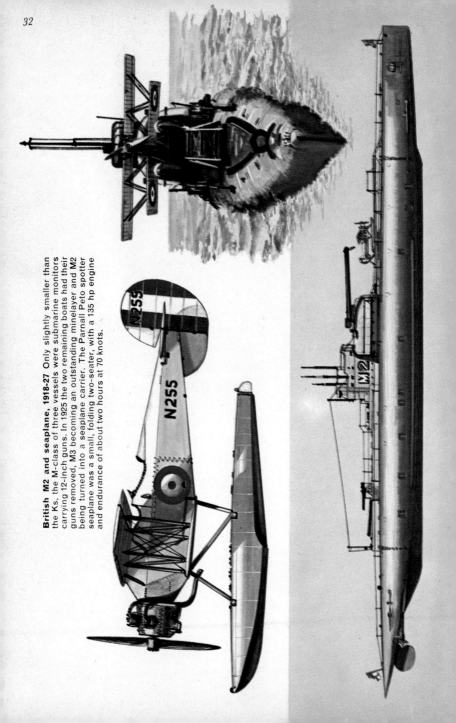

British M2 and seaplane, 1918-27 Only slightly smaller than the Ks, the M-class of three vessels were submarine monitors carrying 12-inch guns. In 1925 the two remaining boats had their guns removed, M3 becoming an outstanding minelayer and M2 being turned into a seaplane carrier. The Parnall Peto spotter seaplane was a small, folding two-seater, with a 135 hp engine and endurance of about two hours at 70 knots.

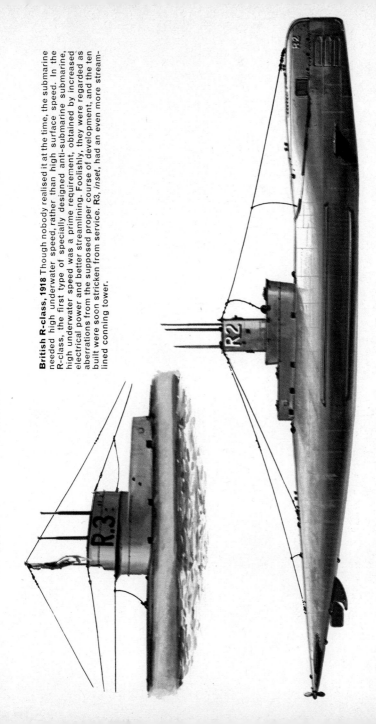

British R-class, 1918 Though nobody realised it at the time, the submarine needed high underwater speed, rather than high surface speed. In the R-class, the first type of specially designed anti-submarine submarine, high underwater speed was a prime requirement, obtained by increased electrical power and better streamlining. Foolishly, they were regarded as aberrations from the supposed proper course of development, and the ten built were soon stricken from service. R3, *inset*, had an even more stream-lined conning tower.

French Redoutable class, 1928 This important class of 1,500-tonners numbered eventually no fewer than 31 submarines, the example depicted being Archimède. These had four big bow tubes; the rest of the tubes were all in revolving mounts on deck, swung out from the superstructure to point at the target. Out of all this big class only one, Casablanca, chose to fight with the Allies in World War II.

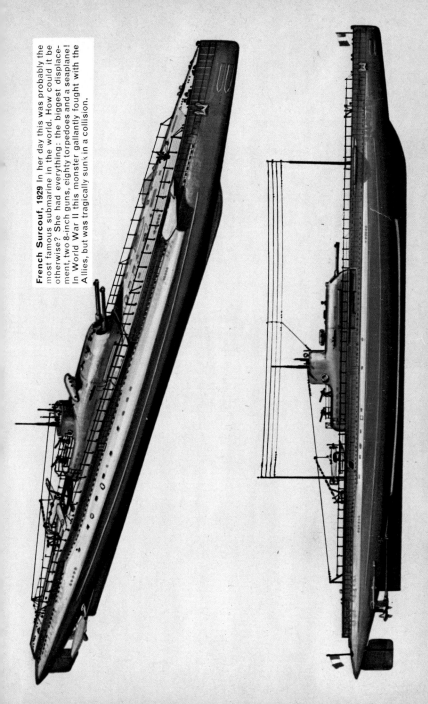

French Surcouf, 1929 In her day this was probably the most famous submarine in the world. How could it be otherwise? She had everything: the biggest displacement, two 8-inch guns, eighty torpedoes and a seaplane! In World War II this monster gallantly fought with the Allies, but was tragically sunk in a collision.

French Junon, 1935 During the inter-war years France never managed to decide on a medium submarine class, building instead small groups of Schneider-Laubeuf, Normand-Fenaux and Loire-Simonot designs. Lack of standardization was an obvious handicap, though they did carry similar armament. Two of these smaller classes provided ships which fought on the Allied side in World War II; Junon was one, the other being Minerve.

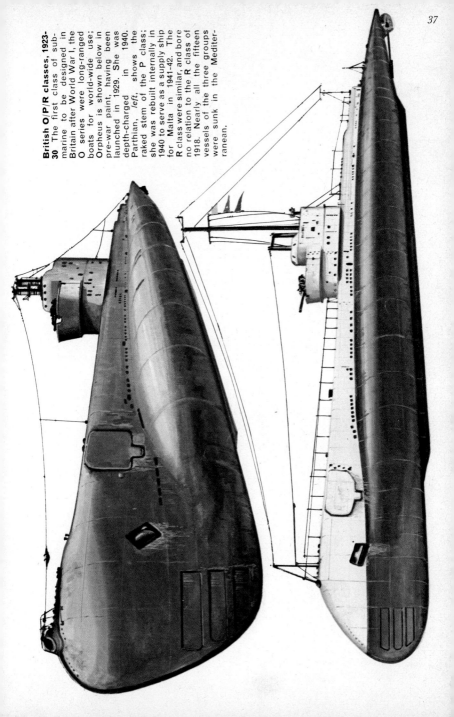

British O/P/R classes, 1923-30 The first class of submarine to be designed in Britain after World War I, the O series were long-ranged boats for world-wide use; Orpheus is shown below in pre-war paint, having been launched in 1929. She was depth-charged in 1940. Parthian, *left*, shows the raked stem of the P class; she was rebuilt internally in 1940 to serve as a supply ship for Malta in 1941-42. The R class were similar, and bore no relation to the R class of 1918. Nearly all the fifteen vessels of the three groups were sunk in the Mediterranean.

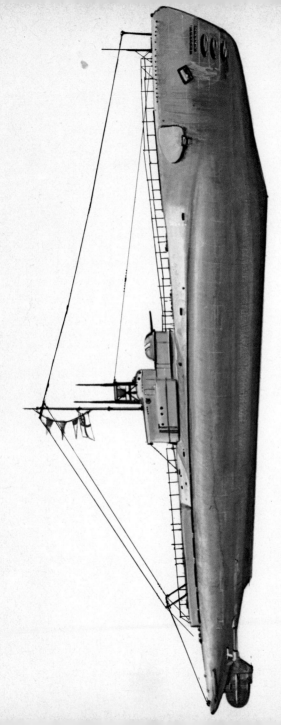

38

British river-class, 1932 HMS Thames, the lead-ship of three of this type, set a speed record for diesel engines of 21·5 knots, and her two sisters were 1 kt faster. These big, long-ranged boats were the final fruit of the Admiralty's wish to build 'Fleet' Submarines. The idea was abandoned only when it was belatedly realised that surface capital ships were capable of 30 knots. In World War II these oceangoing boats were misemployed in the North Sea (where the Thames was mined) and in the Mediterranean. Clyde and Severn reached the Far East in time to be scrapped.

USS Gato, 1941 Side elevation and plan views of the lead-ship of the first big class of US Navy submarine built in World War II. Thanks to methodical and sound development between the wars, the American fleet submarine was by 1941 ideal for the type of work it would have to do. It made no stupid attempt to race with the surface fleet, but had the size and range to undertake long missions in the Pacific and accommodate all the added weapons and radar that experience would show to be needed.

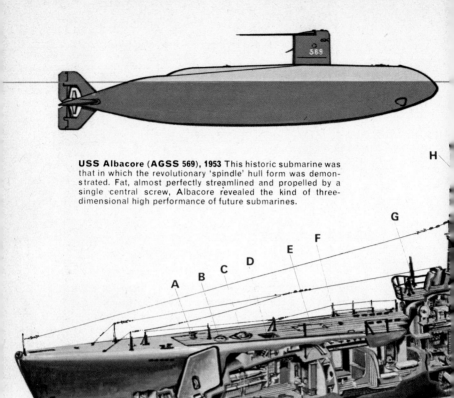

USS Albacore (AGSS 569), 1953 This historic submarine was that in which the revolutionary 'spindle' hull form was demonstrated. Fat, almost perfectly streamlined and propelled by a single central screw, Albacore revealed the kind of three-dimensional high performance of future submarines.

H

G

F

E

D

C

B

A

O

M   N

USS Tench (SS417), 1944 The extent of a typical Guppy post-war rebuild is seen in this side elevation of a submarine which originally looked like that in the main illustration. Internally the Guppy conversions had dramatically increased electric propulsive power.

USS Tang (SS563), 1951 Typical of the first post-war new builds, Tang started from scratch with all the German Type XXI background incorporated, as well as major American improvements in sonar, electronics and countermeasures. Gudgeon of this class is portrayed on a later page.

USS Perch (SS313), 1944 Balao class The cutaway drawing typifies the Fleet Type submarines of the US Navy in World War II. Large and superbly equipped, they were outstandingly reliable, long-ranged and effective fighting vessels. **A** capstan; **B** telephone marker buoy; **C** escape hatch; **D** companionway; **E** torpedo hatch; **F** wardroom; **G** 20 mm AA gun; **H** Nos 1 and 2 periscopes; **J** SD radar; **K** SJ radar; **L** radio compass loop; **M** sonar; **N** forward batteries; **O** 3,000 lb/sq. in. compressor; **P** air conditioning; **Q** ammunition; **R** galley and crew mess; **S** bunks; **T** 5-inch gun; **U** 1,600 hp diesel (four); **V** bilge keel; **W** 1,350 hp electric motor (four).

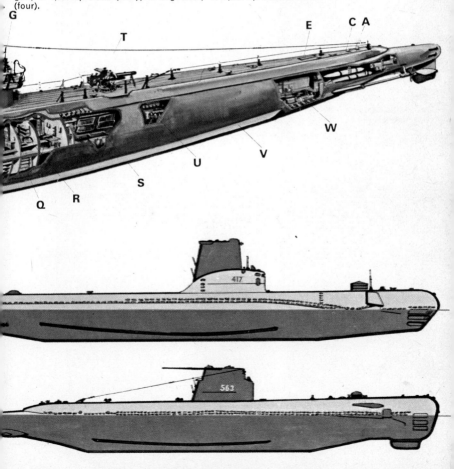

42

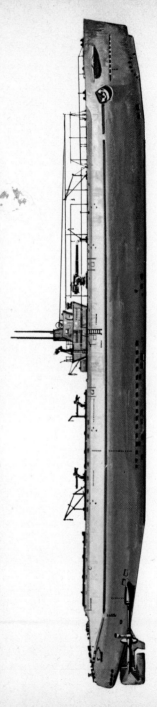

Japanese KD6A (I72), 1935 One of the best types of pre-war Japanese ocean-going submarine, this class of six was one of the few to be aggressively used in the Pacific war and scored many victims including the carrier USS Yorktown.

Japanese D1, 1943 From 1942 onwards the Imperial Navy's submarine service was grossly misused, badly led and no longer capable of powerful aggressive action. Most new construction was halted, except for odd prototypes and, later,

Larger and more powerful than the American Fleet submarines, these formidable vessels would have been a thorn in the Allies' side if there had been more of them, and if they had been fitted with radar.

midgets and suicide craft. An exception was this class of a dozen small boats originally intended for coastal operations. They were completed as transports, with no tubes, to serve beleaguered garrisons.

Japanese Kaiten, 1944 By mid-1944 all normal planning was replaced in Japan by emergency measures. No weapon better typified this than the Kaiten (Heaven Shaker), a manned adaptation of the standard 553 mm torpedo. This torpedo, the Long Lance, was the biggest, fastest and most destructive in the world. Kaiten 1, Illustrated *above*, was succeeded by developments with different engines.

Japanese Koryu D, 1945 This was the ultimate design of midget submarine to go into production in Japan, and it marked a vast advance over the Types A and C. Manned by a crew of five, it had a powerful high-speed diesel, and range over 1,000 miles. Hundreds were made in the final weeks before the Japanese surrender.

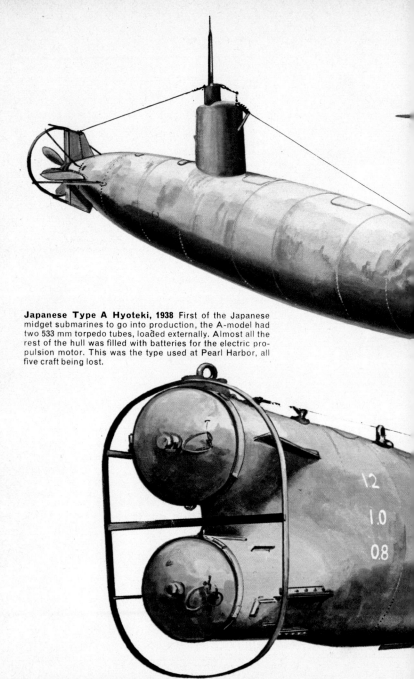

Japanese Type A Hyoteki, 1938 First of the Japanese midget submarines to go into production, the A-model had two 533 mm torpedo tubes, loaded externally. Almost all the rest of the hull was filled with batteries for the electric propulsion motor. This was the type used at Pearl Harbor, all five craft being lost.

Japanese Kairyu, 1945 Though seemingly a midget submarine, the Kairyu (Sea Dragon) was eventually produced as a suicide craft with a devastating warhead in the bows. Few were used in action, and nearly all were left not quite completed.

Japanese Type C Kohyoteki, 1942 Developed directly from the Type A, this slightly larger design had a crew increased from two to three and added a small diesel engine to charge the batteries and thus multiply the radius of action. Only a few were built, the main effort being applied to the bigger Type D and, especially, suicide craft.

Italian Perla, 1935 (*Left*) Unlike most Italian submarines, this vessel had an active wartime career, operating from Bordeaux under German control, surrendering to the Royal Navy and finally serving in the Royal Hellenic Navy! Name-ship of a class of ten, she was smaller than a German Type VIIC and less than half as powerful.

Italian Acciaio, 1941 (*Above*) Another class lead-ship, Acciaio represented the pinnacle of twenty years of Italian development of boats in the 700-ton category. Reference to the data tables shows how little progress was made in those two decades, this final class marking no operational inprovement over the earlier designs (better AA armament was being fitted to all boats at the time of the Armistice in 1943). This view shows the two stern tubes, earlier classes having all six in the bow.

Italian Adua class, 1940 (*Below*) Alagi of this class is typical of the Italian 700-tonners, differing only in detail from the Perla class and from the Sirena of 1933 from which both groups were descended. Though they accomplished far more than the bigger Italian boats, most of Italy's medium submarines spent the war either in port or being scuttled (often before being completed).

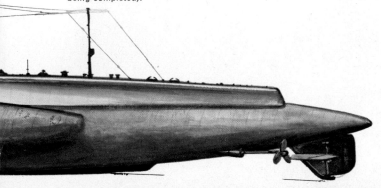

48

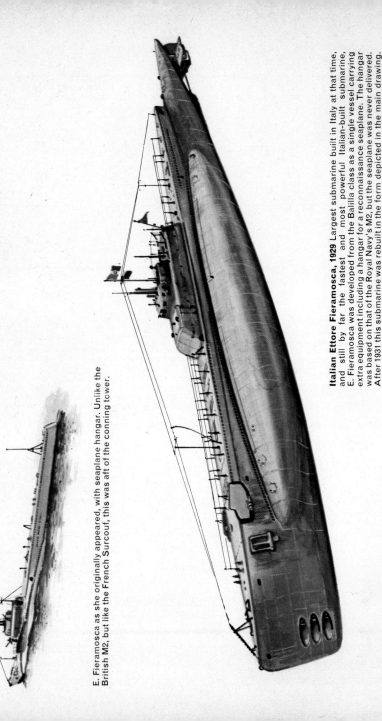

E. Fieramosca as she originally appeared, with seaplane hangar. Unlike the British M2, but like the French Surcouf, this was aft of the conning tower.

Italian Ettore Fieramosca, 1929 Largest submarine built in Italy at that time, and still by far the fastest and most powerful Italian-built submarine, E. Fieramosca was developed from the Balilla class as a single vessel carrying extra equipment including a hangar for a reconnaissance seaplane. The hangar was based on that of the Royal Navy's M2, but the seaplane was never delivered. After 1931 this submarine was rebuilt in the form depicted in the main drawing.

Italian Miale SLC, 1938 (*Left*) Italy pioneered the 'human torpedo' in its non-suicidal form, and despite its name (Miale, Pig) the resulting device was thoroughly effective. Moreover, in sharp contrast to most of the Italian submarine force, these tiny two-man vehicles were used with great skill, bravery and devastating effect.

British Chariot, 1942 (*Below*) Very similar to the Miale, except in that its crew rode on it instead of sitting in it, the Royal Navy's 'human torpedoes' were likewise intended for clandestine attacks on vessels at anchor. Norwegian waters were found to cripple the operators through cold, but in the Mediterranean the Chariots did great work.

German Type IA, 1936 Based on a vessel built in Spain for Turkey, the two Type IIA (U25 and U26) were much larger than the Type II series and eventually led to the slightly smaller Type VII family – built in far greater numbers than any other submarine before or since. The clean exterior of U25, illustrated below, contrasts with the wartime boats with heavy AA armament.

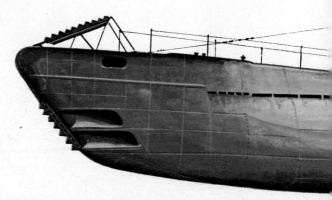

German Type IIB, 1935 The first production type of U-boat for the rebuilt navy of the Third Reich, the IIB (U7-U24) was used mainly in a training role. A few were deployed operationally, with large extensions to the conning tower to carry two pairs of 20 mm AA guns. All these early boats were built at Kiel, four by Deutsche Werke and the remainder by Germania Werft; this was in the days before widespread prefabrication.

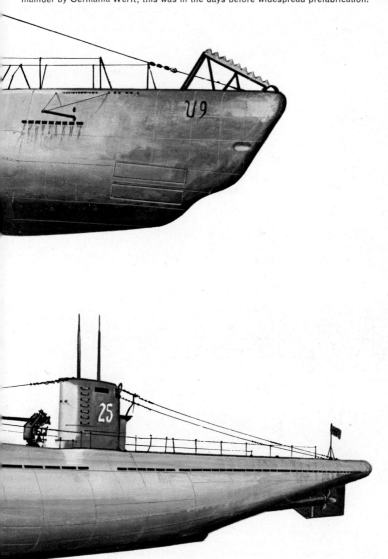

52

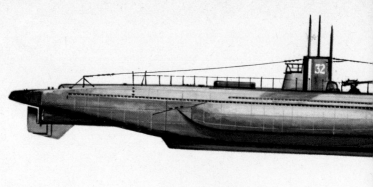

The standard German U-boat of World War II was designed at the start of the Nazi era to be as small as possible, so that more could be built without contravening the London Naval Treaty. One Type VIIA served in the Spanish Civil War (U32, *top*, with German recognition stripes), and this pattern was developed into the VIIC (*right*) which was built in far greater numbers than any other submarine in history. Living in vile and cramped conditions, their skilled and courageous crews made them formidable weapons. By 1943 they had greatly augmented flak (quad and twin 20 mm, *above*) and often fought it out on the surface against hostile aircraft.

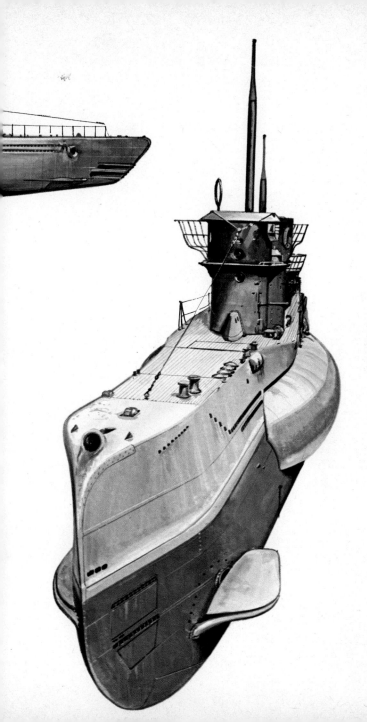

54

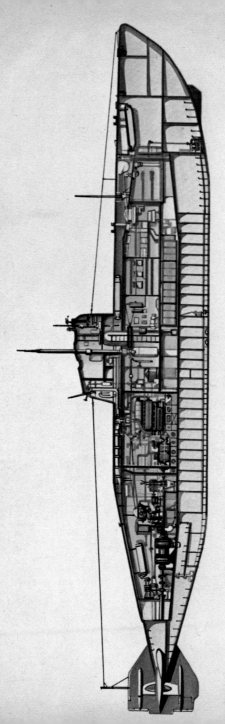

German Type XVIIB, 1944 The original Type XVII, of 1943, was significant in many ways. Not least was its basic design assumption that underwater speed is vitally important; the traditional ratio of propulsive power was radically over-turned, with underwater power 24 times as great as the surface power. In the XVIIB (U1407, later to become HMS

Meteorite, is depicted) a balance was struck between speed, range, striking power and practicality that would have been difficult to counter. The Royal Navy's subsequent attempts to use the radical High-Test Peroxide (Perhydrol) fuel were fumbling and fraught by 'incidents', but in the Type XVIIB fifty tons of it were handled by 1945 in a routine manner.

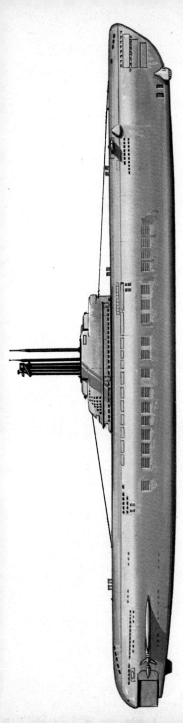

The Nazi Blitzkrieg philosophy made no provision for long war. In May 1943 a tremendous climax in the U-boat war suddenly produced not victory but defeat, and it was realised the Type VIIC was obsolete. Frantically a completely new and infinitely more lethal submarine was designed, the Type XXI, with an underwater speed of 16 knots. Hundreds were laid down in a vast prefab building programme, but the XXI was just too late to hit the Allies. Its main effect in history was to revolutionise post-war submarine design.

German Marder, 1944 This was one of the second-generation German midget submarines, provided with breathing equipment and electric propulsion for prolonged travel under water. A standard G7e torpedo was carried beneath a hull based on the same weapon; about 300 were built.

German Mölch, 1944 From Hecht was derived Neger, with longer range and often with a small petrol engine to charge the batteries. This was refined into the larger Mölch, which also had breathing equipment for submerged operation and carried up to two G7e torpedoes. A few Mölch were used against Allied ships at Antwerp in late 1944.

German Seehund, 1944-45 Last, biggest and possibly best of the German midgets, this 13- to 15-tonner was used in some numbers in 1945, one apparently suffering a 'hung-up' torpedo and shooting at high speed past a British destroyer!

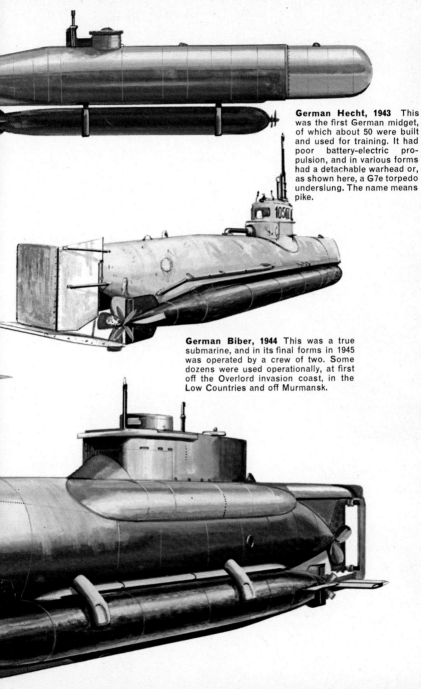

German Hecht, 1943 This was the first German midget, of which about 50 were built and used for training. It had poor battery-electric propulsion, and in various forms had a detachable warhead or, as shown here, a G7e torpedo underslung. The name means pike.

German Biber, 1944 This was a true submarine, and in its final forms in 1945 was operated by a crew of two. Some dozens were used operationally, at first off the Overlord invasion coast, in the Low Countries and off Murmansk.

British S-class, 1931 There is some justification for describing these medium patrol boats as the most important of all the Royal Navy's submarines in the pre-missile era. First ordered in the 1929 Navy Estimates, they were still in production in 1944. It is hardly to be wondered at that it was numerically the largest of all British classes, and almost all gave outstanding war service under the most difficult conditions. They were smaller and had much less powerful engines than the German Type VIIC, yet their fighting efficiency was comparable.

The drawing (*right*) shows HMS Safari, launched in 1941 and for her first 18 months of service known merely as P.62. She typifies the batches built prior to 1943. The upper illustration is of HMS Stonehenge, one of the large third group with a seventh tube added at the stern, fitted with 20 mm AA gun and air-warning radar, and usually with the 3-inch gun replaced by a 4-inch. Later boats also had welded hulls.

The lower drawing depicts HMS Unison, typical of the class as built (four early examples had two external tubes above the bow). The upper depicts Dolfijn, of the Royal Netherlands Navy, with air-warning radar at the upper rear of the conning tower.

British U-class, 1937 Planned as unarmed boats for anti-submarine training, these small and nimble vessels became one of the most important operational classes in World War II, with a record that can fairly be described as heroic. They served with especial distinction in the Mediterranean, where their small size was an advantage, though 14 were sunk in that theatre.

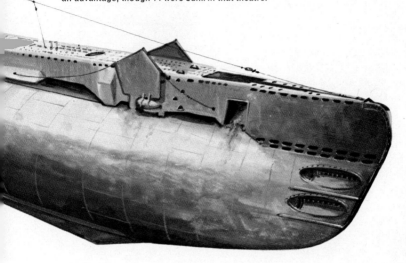

British V-class, 1943 This class of
small patrol submarines differed from
the U-series chiefly in having partly
welded hulls, so that they could dive
100 feet deeper, to 300 feet. Large
numbers were planned, but with the
capitulation of Italy in 1943 the need
was for large boats for use in the Far
East and most V-class construction
was cancelled. The example shown
is HMS Venturer, the lead-ship. After
the war she was transferred to the
Royal Netherlands Navy, and many
other V-class vessels served with
Allied navies during and after the
war.

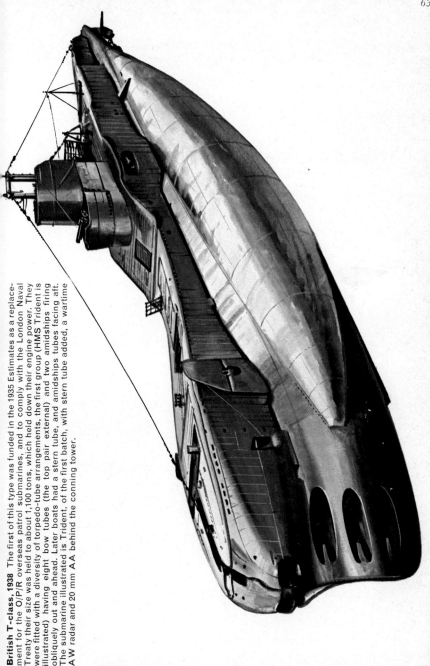

British T-class, 1938 The first of this type was funded in the 1935 Estimates as a replacement for the O/P/R overseas patrol submarines, and to comply with the London Naval Treaty their size was held to about 1,100 tons, which held down their engine power. They were fitted with a diversity of torpedo-tube arrangements, the first group (HMS Trident is illustrated) having eight bow tubes (the top pair external) and two amidships firing obliquely out and ahead. Later boats had a stern tube, and amidships tubes facing aft. The submarine illustrated is Trident, of the first batch, with stern tube added, a wartime AW radar and 20 mm AA behind the conning tower.

USS Gudgeon (SS567), 1952 This member of the Tang class affords an instructive comparison with the lead-ship illustrated on a previous page. Gudgeon, which in 1957-58 became the first American submarine to sail around the world, has three prominent PUFF fins housing BQG-4 sonar, breaking an otherwise clean hull form. These hulls were among the last to be built prior to the introduction of the spindle shape.

USS Barracuda (SS-T3), 1951 This small boat was built as an anti-submarine platform ,with large bulbous bow sonar. In 1959 she was rebuilt as an AS target, though her poor speeds of 10/8 knots reduce her value in this role. She has a pair of 21-inch tubes at each end, and is supposed to have some attack capability, having in 1972 been added to the US Navy's attack force.

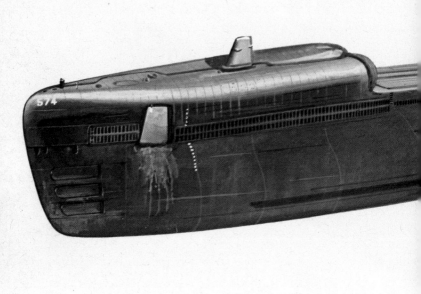

USS Grayback (SSG574), 1958 Originally authorised as an attack submarine, this big pre-nuclear vessel was completed as shown with provision to carry and launch two Vought Regulus I missiles, each of which could carry a large conventional or nuclear warhead about 600 miles in one hour. In 1967-69 she was rebuilt as LPSS574, an amphibious transport. The upper picture shows her thus lengthened by 12 feet, with modified 'hangars' and a third PUFF fin.

68

USS Tigrone (AGSS 419) was the last World War II
submarine to remain in the US Navy, not being stricken
until the summer of 1975. Originally one of the Tench
class, she was rebuilt after the war as a radar picket
(SSR 419), and is seen in this form below with three
surveillance radars and a height-finder radar. In 1959
she reverted to ordinary SS use and in 1963 became an
auxiliary used mainly for research, with a huge bow bin
housing a surface-vessel sonar (right).

69

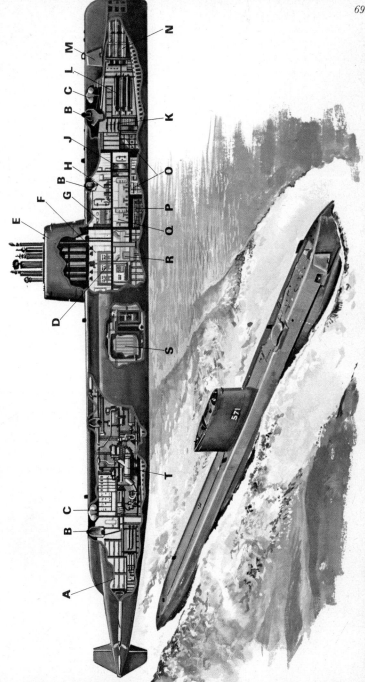

USS Nautilus (SSN571), 1954 One of the most famous submarines in the world, Nautilus was the first vehicle of any kind to be propelled by nuclear energy. **A** aft crew quarters; **B** escape trunk; **C** tethered marker buoy with communications; **D** attack centre; **E** periscopes, radar, snort, communications; **F** periscope room; **G** captain's stateroom; **H** wardroom; **J** galley; **K** for'ard crew quarters; **L** reloads; **M** folded bow planes; **N** six tubes; **O** stores; **P** batteries; **Q** messdeck; **R** control room; **S** reactor; **T** steam turbines (two).

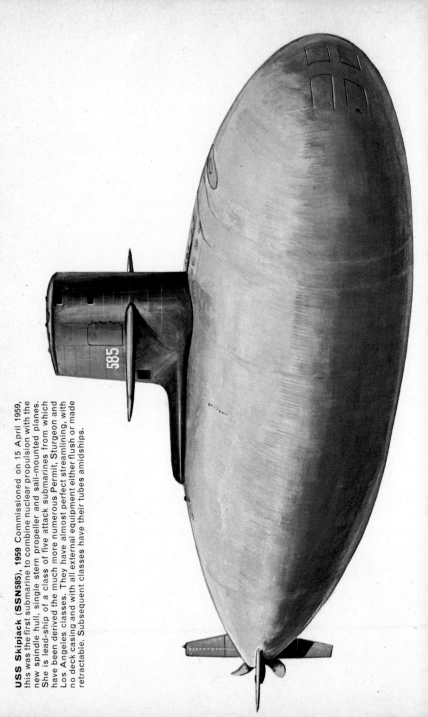

USS Skipjack (SSN585), 1959 Commissioned on 15 April 1959, this was the first submarine to combine nuclear propulsion with the new spindle hull, single stern propeller and sail-mounted planes. She is lead-ship of a class of five attack submarines from which have been derived the much more numerous Permit, Sturgeon and Los Angeles classes. They have almost perfect streamlining, with no deck casing and with all external equipment either flush or made retractable. Subsequent classes have their tubes amidships.

USS George Washington (SSBN598), 1960 Beyond doubt, this was the most revolutionary and portentous warship in history, far exceeding in importance even HMS Dreadnought of 1906 or the first aircraft carriers of 1915. She began as Scorpion, of the Skipjack class, but during construction was cut in two behind the sail, an extra 75 foot

missile section was welded in, and she was hastily commissioned as the first of 41 Fleet Ballistic Missile Submarines – prime carriers of the US nuclear deterrent aimed at possible enemy cities. Though fitted with six bow tubes, they avoid hostile naval forces and serve purely as strategic missile launch platforms.

A single propeller; **B** reduction gear; **C** steam turbine; **D** escape trunk; **E** flat-top decking with eight pairs of inner and outer missile doors; **F** navigation room; **G** bridge; **H** periscope room; **J** control room; **K** wardroom; **L** reload

torpedoes; **M** crew mess; **N** bunks; **O** batteries; **P** intertial gyro room; **Q** missile control centre; **R** Polaris A-3 tubes and Mk 84 ejector system; **S** reactor and heat exchanger.

USS Andrew Jackson (SSBN619), 1963. Third ship of the Lafayette class of Fleet Ballistic Missile Submarines, Andrew Jackson shows the features of these 37 very large vessels which, unlike George Washington, were designed for missile armament from the start. One of these vessels, SSBN626 Daniel Webster, has a large sonar fairing above the bow on which are mounted the planes. The first eight ships were at first armed with Polaris A-2, and the rest with A-3; all are being converted to fire Poseidon.

UGM-73A Poseidon C-3 weighs 65,000 lb and fires up to 14 powerful warheads (said to be of 40 to 50 megatons each), each individually targeted over ranges up to 2,875 miles

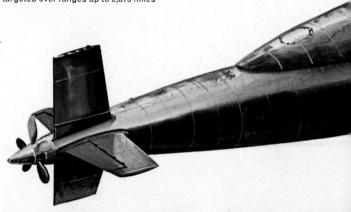

GM-27C Polaris A-3 weighs 35,000 lb and fires three 0.2 megaton warheads up to 2,875 miles.

UGM-27B Polaris A-2 weighs 30,000 lb and fires a 0.5 megaton warhead up to 1,725 miles.

US Trident submarine (SSBN711), 1979 This illustration shows the external appearance of the enormous submarines which the US Navy hopes to buy to continue the undersea missile force after the completion of the 20-year operational life of earlier vessels. With a submerged displacement of some 15,000 tons, they will each carry 24 Trident C-4 missiles having the same diameter as Poseidon but greater length, and sending heavier warheads over ranges up to at least 4,000 miles.

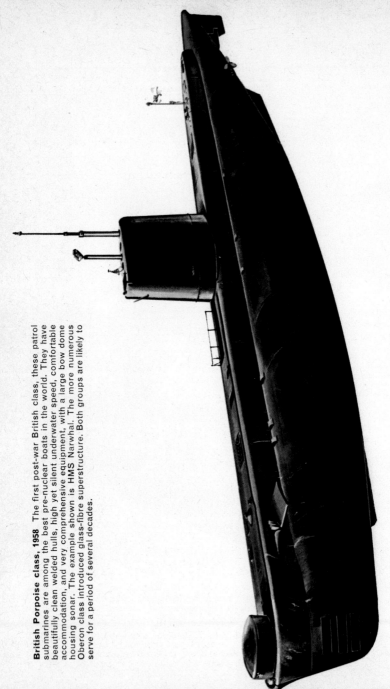

British Porpoise class, 1958 The first post-war British class, these patrol submarines are among the best pre-nuclear boats in the world. They have beautifully clean welded hulls, high yet silent underwater speed, comfortable accommodation, and very comprehensive equipment, with a large bow dome housing sonar. The example shown is HMS Narwhal. The more numerous Oberon class introduced glass-fibre superstructure. Both groups are likely to serve for a period of several decades.

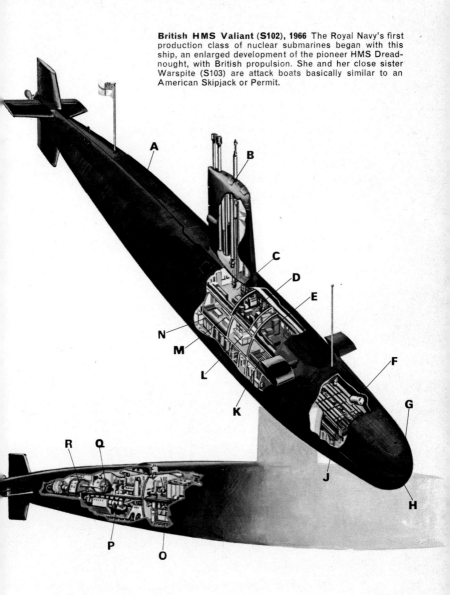

British HMS Valiant (S102), 1966 The Royal Navy's first production class of nuclear submarines began with this ship, an enlarged development of the pioneer HMS Dreadnought, with British propulsion. She and her close sister Warspite (S103) are attack boats basically similar to an American Skipjack or Permit.

A hull prefabricated from heavy ring sections; **B** periscopes, snort and X-band radar; **C** periscope and navigation room; **D** control room (attack centre); **E** wardroom; **F** torpedo hatch; **G** forehead sonar array; **H** six tubes; **J** multiple reloads; **K** crew quarters; **L** galley; **M** messdeck; **N** batteries; **O** reactor room; **P** steam turbines (two); **Q** electric propulsion motors (two); **R** reduction gears to single propeller.

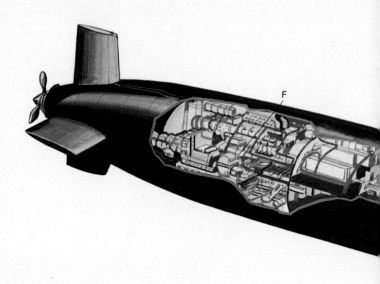

British HMS Resolution (S22), 1967 The four ships of this class were constructed to a priority programme between 1964 and 1969, two by Vickers at Barrow and two by Cammell Laird at Birkenhead. They were originally to have been joined by a fifth, to increase the number always on station from one to two, but this ship was cancelled in 1965. To deliver the British nuclear deterrent they incorporate a missile section similar to that of the Lafayette class, but in other respects differ markedly from the American Polaris vessels. **A** six tubes; **B** eyebrow sonar arrays; **C** missile control centre; **D** periscopes, snort, communications, and X-band radar; **E** missile section; **F** steam turbines (two); **G** inertial gyro room; **H** batteries.

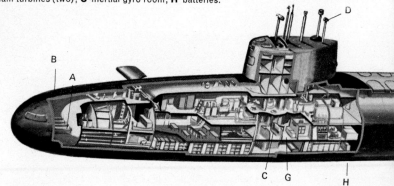

British HMS Swiftsure (S107), 1973 Strictly, the Royal Navy's nuclear attack submarines comprise four groups: Dreadnought (S101); Valiant and Warspite; the three Churchills (S104-106); and the four of this class. The Swiftsure submarines are intended for the same mission as their predecessors, but are redesigned; the hull is of a new, more cylindrical form, giving greater interior volume and lower drag, and the sail is smaller. Details of these ships may not yet be published. **A** control room; **B** wardroom; **C** advanced sonar; **D** four tubes (a fifth is elsewhere); **E** crew deck; **F** modified nuclear propulsion system.

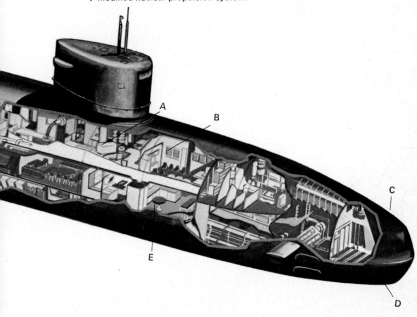

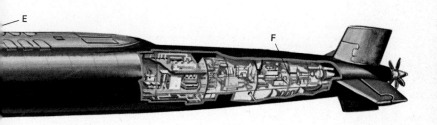

French Aréthuse (S635), 1958 Lead-ship of her class of four
small patrol submarines, this neat boat has proved successful
and troublefree. She has a single diesel-electric set, can dive
to 600 feet and carries eight torpedoes for four bow tubes.

French Gymnote (S655), 1966 This submarine began life as
the first non-American nuclear submarine in 1958. In 1959 this
was cancelled, but the hull was taken over in 1963 and completed
as the experimental and trials submarine for French underwater
equipment then in the design or prototype stage, with particular
emphasis on the MSBS missile system. Powered by two diesel-
electric sets, Gymnote incorporates a missile section with four
MSBS launch tubes from which development or production
missiles can be launched automatically as in the SNLE vessels.

MSBS ballistic missile The original armament of the SNLE
vessels (depicted overleaf) was the M-1, weighing about
39,700 lb and throwing a nuclear warhead up to 1,615 miles. This
has been replaced by M-2, with a more advanced second stage
increasing range to 1,960 miles.

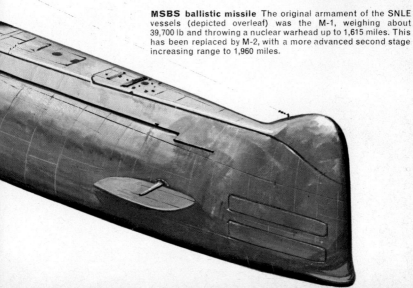

French SNLE Redoutable, 1971. One has only to glance at the hull of this monster ballistic-missile submarine to see that, unlike its British counterparts, it owes little to the US Polaris-carrying SSBN design of 1957. Partly owing to the length of the MSBS missile these hulls are even bigger than those of the US and British vessels, though slightly smaller than the Soviet Yankee and Delta classes. The propeller is driven by a single electric motor supplied by two turbo-alternators drawing steam from the single reactor. The first four SNLE vessels will be in service by late 1976; the fifth will follow in 1978.

French Agosta, 1975 First of four (more may be authorised), this represents the very latest thinking in oceangoing non-nuclear patrol submarines. In the 1,200-ton class, she has a five-blade propeller driven by main and cruise electric motors, for the most silent propulsion; two 850 kW diesel sets charge the 320-cell batteries. In the bows are the four tubes, 20 torpedoes being carried.

A escape trunks; **B** bunks; **C** attack centre; **D** torpedo hatch; **E** upper and lower sonar; **F** planes have fixed and hinged portions; **G** batteries.

Swedish Sjöormen, 1967 Outstanding in cost/effectiveness, this class of modern patrol submarines is entirely Swedish in design and construction. The hull is remarkably short but of the latest hydro-dynamic form, giving a submerged speed of 20 knots. In the bow are the four tubes, as well as an advanced sonar array. In the stern is the electrically driven five-blade propeller, behind the cruciform fins. Diving planes are carried on the narrow sail. The total complement is only 23, indicating the high degree of automaticity, and these boats can dive to 500 feet and remain on patrol three weeks.

Soviet 'Whisky Long-Bin', 1960 There are believed to have been seven of these conversions of the W-class (see overleaf), which, though better than the Twin-Cylinder, are far from ideal. The hull was cut in two and a 26-foot section spliced in which, when mated with revised fore and aft sections, resulted in a ponderous amidships structure housing two superimposed pairs of tubes for N-3 missiles, set at the correct firing angle. All four fire forwards, but the boat must be pointed approximately at the target. Mid-course missile guidance is provided by another platform, such as a Tu-95 aircraft.

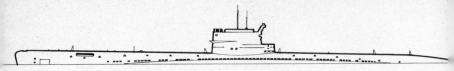

Soviet 'Whisky Canvas-Bag', 1959 Five W-class were
converted as radar pickets, with enormous sails carrying large
surveillance radar aerials. When not in use the aerial was
covered by a 25-foot convas bag, hence the Allied code name.

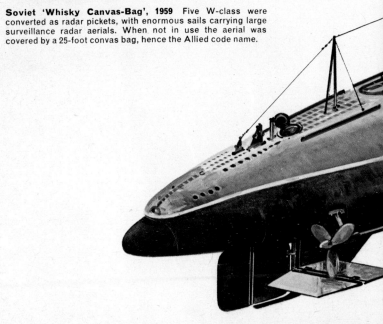

et 'Whisky' class, 1951 By far the most numerous class
ubmarines built anywhere since 1945, these are now being
off or stricken. There were at least eight sub-variants.

Soviet 'Whisky Twin-Cylinder,' 1958 In
order to get the N-3 'Shaddock' missile
aboard a submarine at the earliest date for
trials and training, a small batch of W-class
vessels were fitted with two launch tubes
abaft the conning tower. To fire, the boat is
manoeuvred stern-on to the target and the
missile tube(s) raised. It is thought unlikely
that these clumsy conversions ever achieved
operational status.

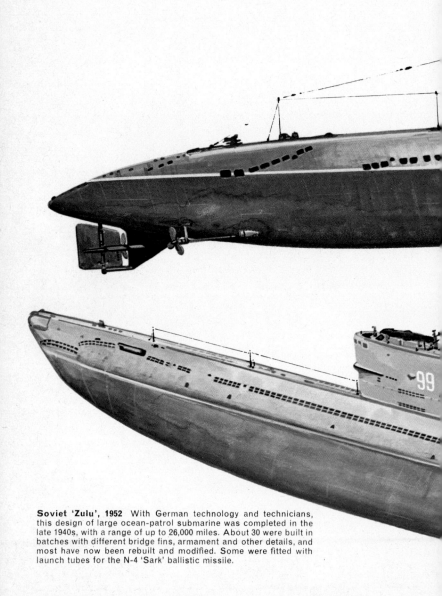

Soviet 'Zulu', 1952 With German technology and technicians, this design of large ocean-patrol submarine was completed in the late 1940s, with a range of up to 26,000 miles. About 30 were built in batches with different bridge fins, armament and other details, and most have now been rebuilt and modified. Some were fitted with launch tubes for the N-4 'Sark' ballistic missile.

Soviet 'Quebec', 1954 The last class of small Soviet submarines, these coastal patrol boats nevertheless have a cruising range of 7,000 miles. It is believed that they were designed to have HTP boost propulsion on the central shaft, but all three screws now have diesel-electric drive.

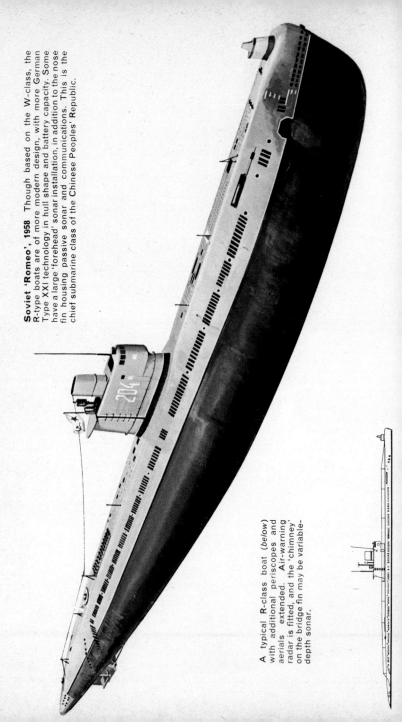

Soviet 'Romeo', 1958 Though based on the W-class, the R-type boats are of more modern design, with more German Type XXI technology in hull shape and battery capacity. Some have a large 'forehead' sonar installation, in addition to the nose fin housing passive sonar and communications. This is the chief submarine class of the Chinese Peoples' Republic.

A typical R-class boat (*below*) with additional periscopes and aerials extended. Air-warning radar is fitted, and the 'chimney' on the bridge fin may be variable-depth sonar.

SS-N-4 'Sark' The first Soviet ballistic missile to be launched by submarines, this was an ungainly solid-propellant weapon 48 feet long and thus needing the full depth of hull and sail (bridge fin). Relatively primitive, it could project a nuclear warhead up to 350 miles, but could not be launched until the submarine had surfaced.

Soviet 'Zulu V', 1956 Seven Z-class submarines were rebuilt in 1955-57 to incorporate vertical launch tubes for the first Soviet naval ballistic missile, the N-4 'Sark'. Though they retained their ten torpedo tubes, the Z V or two were engaged in scientific and fisheries research.

Z5 boats did not appear ever to be fully operational and were used mainly for research and training. Five had been stricken by 1976, and the remaining two were engaged in scientific and fisheries research.

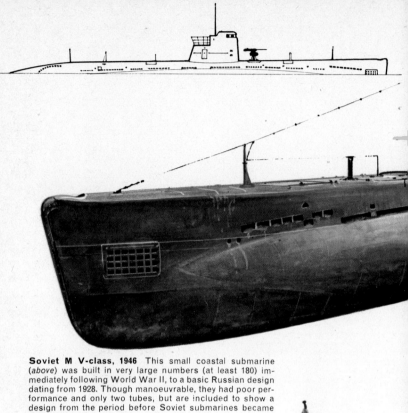

Soviet M V-class, 1946 This small coastal submarine (*above*) was built in very large numbers (at least 180) immediately following World War II, to a basic Russian design dating from 1928. Though manoeuvrable, they had poor performance and only two tubes, but are included to show a design from the period before Soviet submarines became a real menace.

Soviet 'Foxtrot', 1958 Affording a contrast with the little boat above, the F-class (*right*) were one of the most successful Soviet post-war submarine designs, having a hull based on the Z but with more modern propulsion and equipment. At least 56 were built, and they are still encountered all over the world. Some have been sold or given to other navies, including that of India. From the F design were derived other Soviet submarines, notably the G-class illustrated on the following page.

Soviet 'Golf', 1961 About 30 of these missile-firing submarines were built, the design being basically a 'stretch' of the successful F patrol class. The G has possibly the biggest bridge fin ever fitted to a submarine – it is too fat to be called a sail, because its rear portion contains the upper portions of the three large missile tubes.

Originally the missile was the N-4 'Sark', but from about 1967 many G-class boats were converted to fire the much smaller N-5 'Serb' with a range of about 650 miles. Each tube has an inner watertight top closure and a large outer hatch cover, the middle one of which is shown open in the main drawing. N-4 boats are now designated 'Golf I' or G1, and N-5 versions, 'Golf II', or G2.

Soviet 'Juliet', 1962 Though having a totally different hull and propulsion, this class of at least 16 was the logical next generation after the 'Whisky Twin-Cylinder', and 'Long-Bin'. With these formidable vessels four N-3 'Shaddock' tubes were arranged in two pairs pivoted inside the deep hull casing. For firing, the chosen pair is hydraulically raised to the launch elevation of about 18°, with the vessel surfaced but not necessarily at rest. The inset at right shows the tubes of a Whisky Twin-Cylinder. Juliets have an advanced hull form and impressive bow sonar arrays.

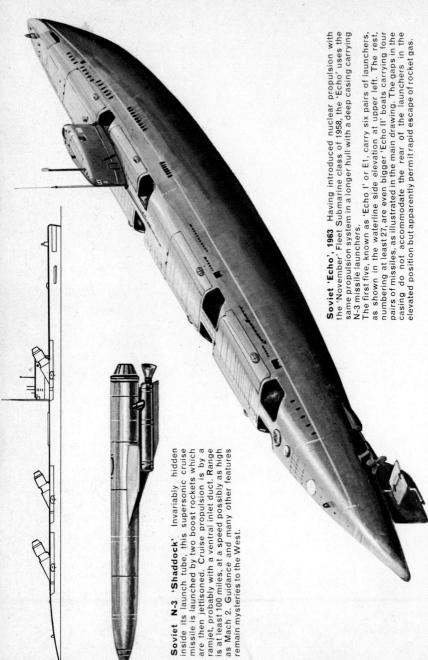

Soviet N-3 'Shaddock' Invariably hidden inside its launch tube, this supersonic cruise missile is launched by two boost rockets which are then jettisoned. Cruise propulsion is by a ramjet, probably with a ventral inlet duct. Range is at least 100 miles, at a speed possibly as high as Mach 2. Guidance and many other features remain mysteries to the West.

Soviet 'Echo', 1963 Having introduced nuclear propulsion with the 'November' Fleet Submarine class of 1958, the 'Echo' uses the same propulsion system in a longer hull with a deep casing carrying N-3 missile launchers.

The first five, known as 'Echo I' or E1, carry six pairs of launchers, as shown in the waterline side elevation at upper left. The rest, numbering at least 27, are even bigger 'Echo II' boats carrying four pairs of missiles, as illustrated in the main drawing. The gaps in the casing do not accommodate the rear of the launchers in the elevated position but apparently permit rapid escape of rocket gas.

SS-N-5 'Serb' Much smaller than the primitive N-4 'Sark', this two-stage solid-propellant missile is expelled from its tube by 18 cold-gas jets built into its base. Range is at least 650 miles, and possibly as great as 1,490 miles. It is believed N-5 can be fired underwater.

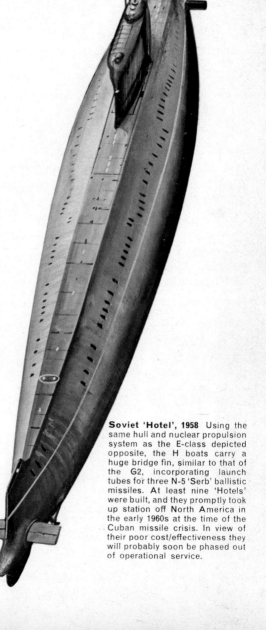

Soviet 'Hotel', 1958 Using the same hull and nuclear propulsion system as the E-class depicted opposite, the H boats carry a huge bridge fin, similar to that of the G2, incorporating launch tubes for three N-5 'Serb' ballistic missiles. At least nine 'Hotels' were built, and they promptly took up station off North America in the early 1960s at the time of the Cuban missile crisis. In view of their poor cost/effectiveness they will probably soon be phased out of operational service.

96

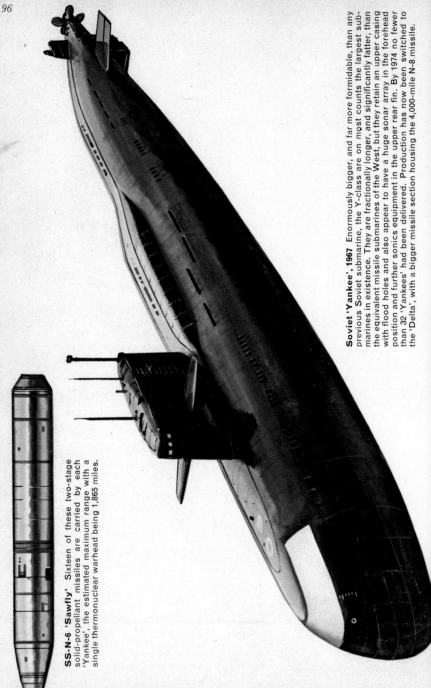

Soviet 'Yankee', 1967 Enormously bigger, and far more formidable, than any previous Soviet submarine, the Y-class are on most counts the largest submarines in existence. They are fractionally longer, and significantly fatter, than the equivalent missile submarines of the West, but they retain an upper casing with flood holes and also appear to have a huge sonar array in the forehead position and further sonics equipment in the upper rear fin. By 1974 no fewer than 32 'Yankees' had been delivered. Production has now been switched to the 'Delta', with a bigger missile section housing the 4,000-mile N-8 missile.

SS-N-6 'Sawfly' Sixteen of these two-stage solid-propellant missiles are carried by each 'Yankee', the estimated maximum range with a single thermonuclear warhead being 1,865 miles.

EARLY SUBMARINES

The submarine, unlike the flying machine, could be constructed and operated with some degree of success centuries ago, when man's technology was by modern standards primitive. Yet, like the flying machine, a bad design could kill its operators, and this was to be proved over and over again. It was only in the final quarter of the nineteenth century that designers began to learn how to make a submarine seaworthy on the surface and stable when submerged. Allied with the emergence of practical internal-combustion engines this made a useful submarine technically possible, and when the new invention of the torpedo was added (and, later, the submarine mine) the way was open to a formidable naval weapon that could sink the biggest battleship without warning.

Drebbel

When one attempts to record technical development more than 350 years ago it is hard to sort truth from fiction. The more one writes, the greater the risk of perpetuating errors, because chroniclers at the time seldom left objective, factual and quantified accounts. What is known beyond doubt is that from about 1600 a Dutch physician named Cornelis Drebbel (there are several variations on the spelling) lived in London and, apparently as a sideline with no thought of either business profit or warlike application, dabbled in submarine navigation.

Essentially his designs were diving bells provided with propulsion by one or more rowers and with a rear rudder for directional control. He built at least three, and not only tested all of them in the Thames but gave numerous public demonstrations. By far the largest, and probably the last, was built in about 1615. She seated twelve rowers in staggered pairs. Between the left and right oarsmen there was room for several passengers, and some contemporary reports claim that King James I travelled submerged in the vessel from Westminster to Greenwich (which is most unlikely, though he certainly watched several of Drebbel's displays, and encouraged the inventor).

One is left pondering many unanswered questions. The main hull structure was hardwood, with a top decking apparently of well-greased leather stretched and pinned over a wooden frame. Presumably the arched roof retained the necessary air, with glass panes sealed into the window apertures. The lower part was open, so that most of each's rower's body was submerged. Buoyancy was varied by goatskin bags, which in some way could be filled with either air or water. But, without drawing in air from above the water surface, the only way of changing the buoyancy would have been to carry air stored under pressure (greater than that of the water at depth) in rigid containers. The problem of rowing effectively under water is self-evident, because on the back-stroke the blade must be accurately feathered edge-on, and even then suffers more drag than in normal rowing. By far the biggest problem of all is: how did Drebbel manage to keep the air fresh during submersions of several hours, as he did? Several accounts claim that he could 'revitalise' the air with 'a few drops' of a secret liquid. We are also left wondering how longitudinal stability was maintained. There was clearly a heavy keel, and a helmsman at the bow whose main task was seemingly to operate left and right hydroplanes. He did not, it seems, have any vision above the water, so navigation is another unexplained problem.

De Son (17)

It is possible that this French entrepreneur was the first person ever to build a submarine intended for use as a warship. He began its construction in Rotterdam in 1653, and not only drawings of it survive but also numerous flamboyant— and quite unrealistic—written claims for its capabilities.

The unnamed craft was built almost entirely of heavy timbers, with a diamond-shaped cross section, length and beam being 72 ft and 12 ft respectively. In the centre was a large paddlewheel, rotated by a 'clockwork mechanism'. At each end there projected a massive horizontal baulk of timber, iron-capped, for use as a battering ram. The crew rode on a platform on top, clear of the water. No evidence survives of any means for controlling ascent and descent, and it seems probable that the vessel was intended to remain permanently awash (though, as the vital crew

would be exposed, the purpose of the immersion of the rest seems obscure). It could have used sails, but De Son stressed the immunity of his vessel to all ordinary hazards, and sails would have degraded this. Contemporary prints show no visible means of controlling direction or trim.

De Son completed his craft, but it apparently refused to move when tested in the water. This is hardly surprising, because, leaving aside the question of the trivial energy that could be stored in clockwork springs, the geometry of the paddle-wheel and its fixed surrounding box is inefficient, and could give little thrust. One contemporary drawing shows a wheel with fixed radial paddles, while another depicts paddles that are clearly hinged and constrained to hang downwards. For a wheel to be effective when totally submerged, the paddles would have to be tilted by a linkage to move broadside-on at the 6 o'clock position and edge-on round the top of the wheel, which is not the case in any illustration of De Son's submarine. Despite this, his creation shows an early attempt to build a lethal submersible warship.

Bushnell's Turtle (18)

David Bushnell was one of the first men to consider himself not as a British colonist in New England but as an American. Around 1760 he studied at Yale and developed a passion for underwater navigation. By 1775 this interest had hardened into an urgent wish to build a submarine weapon that could sink the ships of King George III. With the encouragement of George Washington, Bushnell experimented with mines which could be floated out to enemy ships. He devised heavy iron casks filled with gunpowder and provided either with a slow-burning fuse or a contact-pistol device, so that they would float almost totally submerged and travel out on the tide to a blockading ship. But the problems were obvious, and eventually Bushnell decided he had to build a manned submarine that could transport the charge to the enemy hull and fasten it on.

The result was the Turtle, the first submarine ever used in anger. It comprised left and right turtle-like shells, made of wood caulked and bolted together all round, and with a conning tower at the top provided with a watertight hatch and three glass ports. Inside there was a maze of control levers. One was worked by the feet, and when depressed let water in from below. With the top almost awash, the Turtle would then slowly travel towards the enemy, driven by a hand-cranked screw propeller on the front. When close, the operator would also turn a vertical screw to impart a downthrust, possibly aided by admitting a little more water. There was a depth-gauge, apparently a mercury U-tube, and a compass with phosphorus-paint markings. When under the enemy hull, the operator would screw a vertical auger up into the bottom; then he would release the auger by a special mechanism and leave it attached by a short rope to the 150 lb keg of gunpowder unshipped from the rear and with its fuse linked to a clockwork timing device. The Turtle would then make good its escape, resurfacing at a safe distance and allowing the automatic vent valves to reopen and admit fresh air.

Of course the device needed about three pairs of hands to work effectively, but it was stable and the basis for a successful weapon. On the night of 6 September 1776 Sgt Ezra Lee took Turtle out to the 64-gun frigate HMS Eagle, blockading New York. By sheer bad luck he tried to screw the auger into metal—said to have been a thick strap under the rudder hinge. Failing to get the auger to bite, he eventually had to give up. A British patrol in a rowing boat saw something in the water and gave chase, but turned back when Lee activated the timer, released the charge and caused a huge explosion. This crude submarine did have the effect of making the powerful Royal Navy stand further off-shore and post apprehensive lookouts.

Fulton's Nautilus (19)
Better known for his later work on steam surface vessels, Robert Fulton was an Irish-American who, like Bushnell, longed to bring down the power of the Royal Navy. Aware of Bushnell's work, he conceived something much more like the modern submarine, with a quasi-cylindrical metal hull and rear propeller. In 1797 he took his plan to the French government. Napoleon and the Directory were

interested, but refused Fulton's demand that he or any other submarine crews should be commissioned officers. Agreement was eventually reached, and trials with Nautilus began in 1800. There is justification for considering this the first submarine ever built to government contract.

The ellipsoidal hull had an iron framework covered with copper sheets. Handpumps controlled buoyancy, and propulsion was by a sail on the surface and a hand-cranked propeller when submerged (when the mast was folded back). Fulton and a crew of two went aboard in Le Havre harbour, submerged to a depth of 25 ft for an hour and later covered 1,500 ft (460 m) underwater. Conveyed to Brest, Nautilus was equipped with a detachable 'torpedo' secured to a cable passed through a 'horn' originally mounted above the conning tower from which it could be fastened to the enemy hull. Fulton was anxious to sink a British vessel, but never managed the feat. Though Nautilus was eventually equipped with a compressed-air supply sufficient for 4 hours under water, it could never be manoeuvred beneath an enemy keel, and before long the hull corroded and leaked (possibly because of electrochemical action between the two metals). Fulton fell out with the French and, later, with the British also.

Bauer's Brandtaucher (20)

In 1850 many of the German states were at war with Denmark, and the Danish fleet blockaded the hostile German seaports. At first nothing could be done, but it was a clear case for a submarine and an ex-corporal of the Bavarian Artillery designed one. Wilhelm Bauer called his project Die Brandtaucher (Sea Diver), and he succeeded in obtaining official money and assistance.

His submarine was constructed almost entirely of riveted iron plates on an iron frame. A conning tower surmounted the tall, vertical bow, with a manhole hatch and glass ports on all four sides. A further watertight hatch was—wisely, as it transpired—provided above the stern. The interior, tall enough for most men to stand erect, contained two large treadmill wheels, geared to the stern propeller. Bauer provided the usual water ballast tank and compressed-air supply, as well as a rudder moved by chains from the bow crew-station. Importantly, he also introduced a heavy weight which could be screwed fore and aft to correct trim. This was probably the first submarine built with powerful trimming provisions.

Unfortunately, Bauer had no more success than his predecessors, and almost got drowned into the bargain. On the Brandtaucher's first deep diving trial, in February 1851 in Kiel harbour, the pressure of water on the sides caused them to buckle inwards enough to start a few rivets and begin to flood the interior. The nose dropped, and the weight slid forward, and the submarine sank nose-down on to the bottom. Bauer kept commendably cool. He realised that all that need be done was to let the sea in until the pressure inside was nearly as great as outside. Then the rear hatch could be opened, and a safe exit made. He opened the inlet sea cocks, but his two crewmen thought he had taken leave of his senses. Ignoring his arguments, they knocked him down and sat on him. He went on explaining the situation to them and eventually they understood. They let near-freezing water come in until the pressures were equalised; then Bauer opened the hatch and all three escaped. They had been trapped for five hours.

CSS Hunley (21)

Nearly all the earliest submarines were invented by a beleaguered nation in conflict with a powerful hostile fleet blockading its seaports. In the American Civil War the balance of naval power was enormously in favour of the Union, and the Confederate states were soon being remorselessly blockaded. With cunning, hard work, and plenty of cash, the Confederate forces built or purchased various warships, including a variety of submarines, to try to lift the blockade.

Five experimental submarines were built for the Confederacy in progressively larger sizes by H. L. Hunley. Of the five, only the largest and last, named the CSS Hunley after the inventor, was actually used in combat. An earlier smaller model, the Pioneer, was sunk in Lake Pontchartrain to prevent her from being taken by Union forces.

In 1863, the CSS Hunley was transported by rail from the Gulf Coast, where all the Hunley submarines were built, to the blockaded port of Charleston, South Carolina. Unable to convince the Confederate navy of the potential worth of the vessel, Hunley secured the support of Gen. P. T. Beauregard, and the Hunley was transported and operated by the Confederate army.

An iron tube of elliptical section, the Hunley had a stern screw driven by eight men sitting sideways and working hand cranks. The commander stood at the bow controls and looked through the conning tower; a duplicate station and conning tower were at the stern. A transverse shaft drove left and right hydroplanes to make the zero-buoyant vessel proceed along the surface or, when hear the enemy, beneath it. Equipped with ballast tanks fore and aft, hand-operated pumps, and watertight hatches on the conning towers, the Hunley operated as a true submarine. Plagued by design and operational problems, the ship foundered four times during trials in 1863 and 1864, resulting in the loss of twenty-six lives. One crew was lost when she became stuck in the mud bottom during submergence trials and the air was exhausted before she could be freed. The fourth crew, including the inventor H. L. Hunley, was lost when the submarine was at dockside with the hatches open and was swamped by waves from a passing steamer. Her low freeboard when surfaced, with hatches at bow and stern, made her extremely vulnerable to flooding when pitching.

Early trials were conducted with a torpedo (of a type which would now be classified as a floating contact mine) towed astern. The submarine dived with the intent of towing the torpedo into contact with the target after the submarine had passed under and safely beyond the target. This procedure proved unreliable and the Hunley was fitted with a loose spar carrying a torpedo and a 'harpoon' at her forward end. It was intended that the harpoon would be rammed into the target below the waterline, after which the submarine would back away until it reached the end of a firing lanyard wound on a free-spooling reel mounted on the submarine. The torpedo would then be exploded at a safe distance.

On the evening of 17 February 1864 the Hunley was sent out of Charleston against the 20-gun sloop Housatonic. Infantry-Lieutenant Dixon had a well-drilled crew, a 90-lb (41 km) charge, and great determination. Shut down, the air grew stale; candles burned to give light and to warn of any oxygen deficiency. She went straight to her target, and though seen by the enemy, she was too low in the water for the Housatonic's guns to be trained on her. A mighty explosion sank the sloop, though most of her crew escaped.

But following the action, no sign of the Hunley could be found. Years later it was learned that after she had rammed the sloop, she, too, had been pulled down to a watery grave. When she was finally discovered—about 100 feet from the Housatonic—she was still pointing toward her foe.

Le Plongeur

This remarkable vessel marked a quantum leap forward in submarine design and construction. It was the first official naval design, all previous craft having been the brain-child of a single inventor. It was much larger than earlier submarines, and remarkably similar in essentials to a modern design. It incorporated a specially devised underwater propulsion system.

The plans were drawn up in the French Ministry of Marine by Brun and Bourgeous (or Bourgois) in about 1856–58. The hull was an interesting shape, being a blend between surface seaworthiness and submerged hydrostatic pressure. The ambitious size, which was not to be exceeded for half a century, was partly accounted for by the chosen propulsion system. The 80 h.p. engine, which drove a single screw and was used at all times the vessel was under way, was driven by compressed air. To store this, very large steel bottles were needed, occupying the whole forward part of the hull. This air was also used to blow the ballast tanks and help provide fresh air for crew breathing. A further device actuated by the air supply was a mechanical method of adjusting displacement when close to zero buoyancy. In the upper central part was a crew compartment inside a raised turtle deck, with glass portholes and a cylindrical conning tower. On the bow was a long spar torpedo.

Unfortunately, this impressive and otherwise promising vessel was marred by the fatal weakness that plagued other submarine designers at this time. As soon as buoyancy was reduced to zero, so that Le Plongeur sank beneath the surface, she became longitudinally uncontrollable, pitching wildly like a porpoise. Her pitch correcting system, with powerful stern hydroplanes, did no good at all; indeed, it is possible that, by applying corrective forces that were delayed and out of phase, the hydroplanes were partly the cause of the wild pitching. Nothing in the published record suggests that the trouble could not have been corrected, but the French Navy quite soon abandoned the project and lost interest in submarines.

USS Holland (22)

John Holland, who perhaps more than any other individual can be called the inventor of the modern submarine, was an American of Irish birth who, like previous submarine promoters, hated the power of the Royal Navy. He designed a submarine in 1874, had it rejected by the Navy Secretary in Washington in 1875, and then spent seven years developing Holland I and Holland II for the fanatically anti-British Fenians. In 1883 this Irish revolutionary society lost patience at the long development and towed Holland II away (soon discovering they did not know how to operate it). Five years later the US Navy invited inventors to submit plans for submarines.

Holland's design was judged best, but none of the submissions had any chance of meeting the (then impossible) specified speed and range. He won a second competition in 1893, was eventually awarded $150,000 and worked on USS Plunger, a large steam/electric submarine which again attempted to meet impossible requirements.

In 1896 Holland took a very bold decision. He could see Plunger could not be a success, and he returned the $150,000. With no authority from the Navy, he quickly designed what he considered a much better submarine. His many years of practical experience made him uniquely able to do this, and Holland emerged in 1898 as the first wholly successful submarine in history. Much smaller than the clumsy Plunger, it was powered on the surface by one of the new Otto-cycle i.c. engines burning petrol (gasoline), thus giving much greater power for less installed bulk and without the unpleasant furnace. This engine could be coupled to an electric generator to recharge the batteries that supplied the electric motor that propelled the Holland when submerged. In the bow was a launch tube for one of the new Whitehead torpedoes. Most important of all, Holland knew how to make a submarine behave properly, with the capability of submerging or surfacing rapidly upon command and of running under water at a chosen depth without porpoising up and down.

Holland's gamble paid off. At

first incensed, the Navy were presented with a *fait accompli*. They had the sense to appreciate that the Holland was far superior to the Plunger, and the latter was abandoned. After long and searching trials, the Navy accepted the boat on 11 April 1900. Holland was once more awarded $150,000, and received orders for seven more submarines. Eventually Holland had to sell out to a new company, the Electric Boat Co., which has ever since (and especially since 1950) been a world leader in submarine design and construction. In late 1900 the Holland design was adopted as the first submarine for the Royal Navy; after placing an order with Electric Boat, the decision was taken to build the five submarines in Britain, by Vickers. Thus British designers swiftly caught up with the technology of the submarine, and produced the A-class.

The first US Navy batch were also called the A-class, after the lead ship Adder; the seven were ordered in 1901 and delivered (five from Nixon's yard) in 1902–3. They were slightly larger (64 ft) than Holland.

Narval (23)

Despite the French Navy's rather short-sighted abandonment of Le Plongeur, France gained a world lead in submarines in the last quarter of the nineteenth century. This stemmed from Goubet, a small two-man craft named after its inventor in 1887, which fired the public imagination. It was followed

by the much better Gymnote of 1888, designed by Dupuy de Lome and modified by Gustave Zédé, which was beautifully streamlined and driven by a powerful electric motor. In 1893 followed the much larger Gustave Zédé, which can fairly be described as the first successful submarine to be ordered by a navy and put into operational use. Over the years this vessel was much improved, but it continued to be limited in range because it could not recharge its batteries at sea. The same shortcoming restricted the value of Morse, launched in 1899.

Sensing French superiority, and having no inbuilt reservation about the value or ethics of submarines, the French Marine Minister held a design competition in 1896. It was won by Max Laubeuf, whose Narval was completed in late 1899. This vessel deserves recognition on several counts. It had dual propulsion, the steam engine conferring the outstanding surface speed of 11 knots (20·4 km/hr) and being capable of recharging the electric batteries. It behaved excellently, both on the surface and submerged. Most important of all, the hull comprised an inner pressure envelope of circular section surrounded by an outer hull very like those of high-speed torpedo boats of the time, with good seakeeping qualities. The space between the two, amounting to no less than 41 per cent. of the displacement, was occupied by the water ballast tanks, which were filled or emptied to make the submarine submerge or surface. This hull form has many other advantages, and it soon became standard. Narval's only serious shortcoming was her steam boiler, which made the process of diving take at least 12 minutes and still roasted the interior even after the fire was drawn.

Protector (24)

One of the few submarine builders of the nineteenth century to have (at first) no thought of creating a warship was the young New Yorker Simon Lake. His objective was just to explore the sea and its bed, and his first submarine, Argonaut Jr, was an unpretentious device looking like a large wooden box with wheels. Lake and a friend enjoyed complete success with this entirely successful vehicle, which was really a diving bell equipped with hand-cranked wheels for exploring the bed of New York Bay. It had an air-lock, so that occupants wearing diving gear could step outside and collect objects of interest. By 1897 Lake had completed the much bigger Argonaut, with a metal hull of circular section around which he later built a second, ship-like hull, to give both better seaworthiness when surfaced and a large ballast tank space to control diving and underwater trim.

Perhaps inevitably, Lake eventually had to consider warlike submarines in a search for official sponsors and funds. He proposed a design for a minelaying and mine-sweeping vessel to the US Navy, suffered a flat rejection, and then looked for customers overseas. He

designed Protector and in 1902 sold it to the Imperial Russian Navy, subsequently delivering four more in 1903. Like his earlier craft it was stumpy in appearance and still retained wheels for use on the sea-bed, though they were mechanically propelled and retractable into recesses in the hull. The circular section pressure hull terminated in a point at the bow forming a useful ram, and was surmounted by a second hull with ballast tanks between. Propulsion was by petrol engine on the surface and electric motor submerged. Surprisingly, Lake did not fit Protector with his pioneer 'Schnorkel' system—successfully tried with Argonaut—comprising a flexible air inlet pipe supported on the surface by a buoy, towed by the submarine, which allowed the petrol (gasoline) engine to be used below the surface. Protector had Whitehead torpedo tubes at bow and stern, but was never used in action.

British Holland, A, B, C and D classes (25)

Throughout the nineteenth century the British Admiralty steadfastly professed total disinterest in the submarine. The word disinterest should perhaps be 'negative interest'. Their Lordships had never seen any reason to disagree with their predecessors who had told Fulton (p.99) that the submarine implied 'a mode of warfare which those who command the seas do not want, and which, if successful, would deprive them of it.' In any case, the submarine was a base and inhuman proposition, which no decent officer or gentleman would consider for a moment.

But over a period of years even the British outlook can change. It was principally Isaac Rice who in early 1900 succeeded in making the Admiralty change its mind, and at the industrial level he concluded an agreement between Electric Boat and the famed British arms firm of Vickers Sons & Maxim, at Barrow-in-Furness, Lancashire. Vickers bought a licence to make submarines according to Electric Boat patents, and to have sole rights to the Holland-type boats throughout Europe. In December 1900, less than a year later, the Admiralty ordered five Holland-type boats from Vickers and began training submarine crews. This was the beginning of work that was to make Vickers, Barrow, the only centre in the world with an expertise, design and construction record to rival Electric Boat itself. It was also the beginning of the unsurpassed traditions of the RN Submarine Service, which by 4 August 1914 was by far the biggest in the world.

The first five Hollands were small and limited, but nevertheless practical weapons. Numbered Holland I to V they established the tradition that submarines, though possibly worth having, were not proper ships worthy of bearing names. They proved easy to handle under water and were remarkably effective, but on the surface they were poor sea-boats in rough weather. The submarine crews thus welcomed the commissioning of A1 in July 1903. This boat had been bought at the same time as the five Hollands, and was larger and better in a heavy sea. New features included a conning tower and twin bow tubes arranged side-by-side. Three more were quickly ordered, but the Navy had much to learn and three of these first four A class were lost in collisions. In 1902 nine more were ordered, shorter but fatter and with more powerful petrol (gasoline) engines (petrol-engined submarines were unique in that every other vessel in the fleet burned coal). All save A13 were in service by September 1905; the late delivery was commissioned in 1908 with a heavy oil engine similar to those used in German submarines (not a diesel).

Between April 1905 and March 1910 Vickers built eleven B class—larger, and with a proper deck along the hull—and the unprecedented total of thirty-eight C class submarines with further detail improvements. The latter were successfully used to torpedo U-boats lured by a trawler to which the British submarine was tethered. With the D class the submarine took a large leap forward in capability and in stature. Even as late as 1907 many (perhaps most) of the senior officers of the Royal Navy regarded the submarine as akin to cars and flying machines: newfangled, not a fit thing to be seen with, and quite likely to be a flash in the pan that would wither and soon be forgotten. They called the A, B and C classes 'Fisher's toys' after the architect of Royal Naval supremacy in the final years of peace, Admiral of the Fleet Sir John Fisher, First Sea Lord. But with the D class came the first submarine able to range the open ocean. Carrying fuel for this task had been a daunting prospect in the era of petrol (gasoline) engines, but the D had two diesel driven screws. It had saddle-type ballast tanks, superimposed bow tubes and a stern tube, was almost twice the displacement of its predecessors, and was in all respects a fine seagoing submarine that could do much more than lurk in the shallows off a friendly or enemy shore.

D1, ordered from Vickers in 1907, was actually designed by the Admiralty, as were the Royal Navy's surface fighting ships. Eight were built, D4 being the first to carry a gun. Their successful operation led to the class which did more than any other to win World War 1, the E class.

German U1 (26)
Though the famed Germania yard at Kiel built three Karp class submarines for Russia in 1904, the Imperial German Navy did not order an Unterseeboot until 1905, and the lone U1 was completed the following year. This father of all the U-boats was outstanding for its day, being notably in advance of the contemporary British types. It had a double hull of excellent hydrodynamic form, twin screws with heavy-oil/electric drive, and was generally surprisingly reliable. U1, which served as a training ship in

World War 1, was followed by three larger boats in 1908–9, and then by the important Desiderata class (U5–U18) of 1910–12, which were in front-line use throughout the war. By far the most notable exploit of these early boats was the encounter by U9 (Kapitan-Lt Weddigen) of three British heavy cruisers on 22 September 1914.

Largely because of the decision of the cruisers to stop and help each other, perhaps under the impression they had encountered a minefield, U9 succeeded in sinking all three, sending 3,600 men to their deaths. Then she was able to limp away on her last dregs of battery power, with foul air and unable to charge her batteries, yet succeeded eventually in returning to Wilhelmshaven. More than any other event in history, this totally one-sided action showed in the most dramatic manner that the submarine was not a fragile toy but a terrifyingly lethal weapon against which no vessel was safe.

British E class (27)
Some would claim that this was the first type of submarine to be a truly formidable, reliable and thoroughly developed weapon. Vickers built all the lessons learned from the four previous Royal Navy classes into its design, and also took a natural step forward in size and capability. Today we should judge them small steps, but to the already experienced crews of the Submarine Service— an élite and somewhat separate body of men, who describe their calling as 'The Trade'—the E was

impressive indeed. It introduced a stronger hull, with transverse bulkheads. It had two bow tubes, one at the stern and one firing abeam on each side, spanning the bulged lateral tanks. Ahead of the conning tower was a 12-pdr gun, the installation in D4 having demonstrated its worth. Six of the E class were the first minelayers. Propulsion was by two 800 h.p. diesels, each driving its own screw, giving excellent surface performance. Submerged, the electric batteries were very rapidly exhausted if maximum current was drawn, but at low speed the E class could travel 120 miles under water.

The E was the latest class available at the outbreak of World War 1. It became the most important type of Allied submarine, not only because of numbers, but because of the skill, professionalism and sheer courageous daring of the E class crews. Of fifty-six built for the Royal Navy, eighteen were constructed by Vickers at Barrow, two by Beardmore and fitted out at Barrow, six by HM Dockyard at Chatham and the other thirty by twelve newcomers to the field of submarine construction. Barrow also built AE1 and AE2 for the Royal Australian Navy. Nearly all the Es had been delivered by the end of 1916. One, E22, operated for a time as the world's first aicraft-carrying submarine, with a hanger for two Sopwith Schneider float-seaplanes. Though only nine of the class were in commission in August 1914 they were the first of the seventy-six submarines in the Royal

Navy to draw blood. On 13 September Lt (later Admiral) Max Horton's E9 sank the German cruiser *Hela* off Heligoland; on his next patrol he sank destroyer S116. He introduced the flying of the Jolly Roger (with 'campaign bars') on return from a patrol.

E class submarines did fantastic work in the North Sea and Baltic but, for sheer sustained excitement, nothing could equal the exploits of Lt-Cdr Martin Nasmith's E11 in the Dardanelles campaign. AE2 was early on the scene of this unfortunate operation, but was soon sunk. Then, on 28 April 1915, E14 (Lt-Cdr Boyle) managed to break through the nets and mines in the Dardanelles and terrorised shipping in the Sea of Marmora. E11 followed on the night of 19 May, by which time the narrows were stiff with defences. It was almost beyond the capability of an E to run the 35 miles submerged against the 4-knot current. It was impossible at full power, and at reduced power the trip took 20 hours, close to the submerged limit. Both shores were bristling with Turkish batteries, gunboats swarmed on the water, and below were successions of nets carrying mines. Nasmith's subsequent adventures are perhaps the most thrilling in the history of submarine warfare. He set his torpedoes to float if they missed in the open sea, and it was his practice whenever possible to recover them, temporarily remove the firing pistol and reload them. On his second patrol, having run the gauntlet of even stronger defences, he was bombed by a Turkish seaplane on 6 August 1915, the first aerial ASW operation on record. On the following day E11 shelled Turkish land forces, and First Lieutenant D'Oyley-Hughes went ashore and, between hair-raising brushes with Turkish troops, set charges and blew up the main railway to the Dardanelles.

In November E11 was back again, this time running the gauntlet of the enemy submarine UB14, which had been transported overland and launched into Marmora to hunt down the British raider. Altogether Nasmith (by now Nasmith, VC) spent 96 days in the hostile sea, destroying 101 enemy ships.

German U19 class

Known as the Mittel-U type, this important series of small batches, numbered U19–22, 23–26, 31–41, 43 (no No 42) –50, 51–56, 57–62, 63–65 and 66–70, represented a natural growth and refinement, and were significant in their increased reliance on deck guns to sink ships not worth a costly torpedo. Guns were always at least 88 mm (3·45 in.) and often 105 mm (4·1 in.) calibre, and the torpedo tubes were increased in calibre to 500 mm (19·7 in.), the usual tube disposition being two at each end (U66–70, ordered by Austria, had five of the old 450 mm tubes, four being in the bow). Modifications were introduced after 1915 to enable submarines to pass more readily through net defences. Whereas the bulk of these sub-marines were completed with almost vertical bows, many were modified with sloping shark-head bows, with a net-cutter above. All were refitted with stout jumping wires to lift nets over the conning tower.

German UB classes

Designed for coastal use in the Baltic, North Sea and Mediterranean, this was the most diminutive class of U-boats in World War 1, and was started with the UB I type (UB1–17) which were small and far from potent. Powered by a heavy-oil (not diesel) engine of only 60 h.p. driving a single screw, these baby boats had two of the old 450 mm tubes and were slow and short-ranged. UB10, 12, 16 and 17 were rebuilt as minelayers, with eight mines dropped from four chutes. Most of these boats, like several other U-boats, were sent in pieces to Pola (Adriatic) and Antwerp for assembly. Much more important, the UB II type (UB18–47) had twin diesels, larger tubes (500 mm) and a gun. By 1917 the still larger UB III class (UB48–155) was in production with surface displacement over 500 tons, powerful twin diesels and five 500 mm tubes. These coastal boats were at least as powerful as the standard U-boats had been at the start of the war.

German UC classes   (28)

The first submarines in history ordered as minelayers were the first UC class of small coastal mine-layers designed in late 1914. This class, UC1–15, were simple and planned for fast production. They were powered by old heavy-oil (not diesel) engines of 90 h.p., and so had poor speed. Each had six sloping mine tubes, and no other armament. But the UC II class (UC16–79) of 1916 were larger and carried not only the six tubes, with eighteen mines, but also torpedoes and a gun, and were considerably more powerful with modern diesels. In December 1916 UC19 became the first victim of a depth-charge attack. The final coastal minelayers, the UC III series (UC90–114) (no UC80–89), were of almost 500 tons and further improved.

German UE class

This significantly increased the lethality of the German undersea campaign, because these submarines were long-ranged ocean minelayers able to sow fields up to 1,000 miles from base. The UE I series (U71–80) entered service from 1915, and it is generally believed that it was a mine from one of these that sank the cruiser Hampshire on 5 June 1916 off the Orkneys, with Lord Kitchener (British warlord) on board, in an area where no mines were expected. In 1918 the considerably larger and more powerful UE II class (U117–126) came into use, able to range much further afield and sow no fewer than forty-eight mines. Throughout the war German mines were extremely lethal, in contrast to those of the Allies which (at least at first) generally failed to detonate. It is almost certain that U-boat losses due to mines were mainly due to accidental encounter with their own

mines and not to fields sown by the Allies.

German UA class

In 1916 Germany brought into use a novel vessel, the Deutschland. This was not, as might be imagined, a battleship but a large merchant submarine designed to beat the British blockade. Before 1917 she had twice been to the United States. On each outward journey she carried dyes and other specialised German exports, while on the return she was packed with such vital materials as nickel and rubber which were almost unobtainable in Germany. She gained propaganda success as well, cruising most of the time at 12 knots on the surface on her small 800 h.p. diesel. Later she became U155, and other merchant cruisers—officially classed as Handels U-boote—were numbered U151–157.

These were by no means the largest U-boats, however. In early 1918 deliveries began of the first built as UA (cruisers) proper, intended to wage war off the coast of North America. The first batch (U135–138) were outstanding vessels, with 3,500 h.p. on two screws and a surface displacement of almost 1,200 tons. They had four large tubes and also a 150 mm (5·9 in.) gun. U139–141 were even larger, with six tubes and two 150 mm guns, and U142 was bigger still. It was indeed fortunate that these extremely formidable long-range submarines were not brought into use earlier. Their design strongly influenced the Type IX series in World War 2.

British H class (29)

In November 1914 Charles M. Schwab of the giant US Bethlehem Steel Corporation, returned from Britain with an urgent order for twenty submarines. He turned this over to Electric Boat. To avoid neutrality restrictions, parts for ten (later twelve) were sent for assembly at Canadian Vickers at Montreal, being completed in the record time of six months; the other eight languished at the Fore River Yard at Quincy until the United States entered the war in April 1917. At first the twelve H class were treated by the Royal Navy with caution, but these small boats of a new design proved tough and useful. All were delivered in 1915 under their own power to the Baltic or Mediterranean, and H1 penetrated to Constantinople. Italy bought eight, and the Royal Navy eventually ordered a further thirty-two of the improved H21 type from British yards, with slightly greater displacement and 21 in. tubes. In 1923 H23 tested an experimental Asdic (sonar) above the hull, later fitted to surviving L class as standard.

British L class

The natural successors to the E class as the mainstream of British development, the L was a traditional Admiralty saddle-tank design with larger dimensions and higher performance. They were delivered in three sub-types, and L11, 12, 14,

17 and 25 were minelayers armed with a row of vertical tubes for eight mines on each side amidships. Most of the class were delivered after the Armistice, and survived into the 1930s. A distinctive feature was the large conning tower, with a 4 in. gun at each end.

British K class (30)

It was only to be expected that, with a weapon as radically different as the submarine, there would be disagreement over how it should best be used, and that in many cases painful lessons would have to be learned 'the hard way'. Few of these fundamental problems were quite so serious and long-lasting as the notion of the 'fleet submarine'. Today it is less easy to comprehend why it should ever have been entertained at all, but early in the century the central feature of naval power was a grand fleet of large and small surface vessels steaming along at high speed hoping to make contact with an enemy fleet. To some at the Admiralty it seemed natural to use at least some submarines as an additional part of such a fleet, travelling with it on the surface and then submerging and doing its work.

There were two basic difficulties. The most obvious was that even at this time the battle speed of the fleet, except in the most severe weather, was 24 knots (28 m.p.h.), and no submarine had yet been built to travel at such a speed. Indeed, it was (probably correctly) judged at that time to be beyond the capability of diesel propulsion, and the only answer seemed to be steam turbines. Thus, such a fast submarine was right back with the problems of steam boilers, with their large air consumption, delay in diving and severe heat output when submerged. The second major difficulty was that surface units found it hard to tell a friendly submarine from a hostile one—just as in a later war they could never tell a hostile aircraft from a friendly one, and so fired at all of them—and from the very first exercises involving both surface vessels and submarines it was obvious that the submarine risked being destroyed by its own side unless it kept right out of the way.

Despite these formidable problems their Lordships insisted on building 'fleet submarines'. HMS Swordfish, of 1916, had powerful 3,750 h.p. steam turbines, with boilers and furnace uptakes to a funnel which could be collapsed and sealed ready for diving. The vessel took far too long to dive, and suffered severe explosions due to steam and the electric power. Judged a failure, in 1917 she was converted to a surface ship. This merely whetted the Navy's appetite, and led to vast expenditure on the K class submarines, the biggest and fastest ever seen. Technically they were splendid; at least, they learned from the lessons of earlier attempts, and had many good features. For harbour and inshore propulsion they used their diesel-electric sets, but for cruising with the fleet they ran at 24 knots on 10,500 shp oil-fired steam turbines. Thanks to

clever design they could submerge much faster than any previous steam submarine, but by modern standards the delay was still impossibly long. They were originally flush-decked, and tended to dive into the ocean, so they were rebuilt with large clipper bows with buoyancy tanks above; at the same time the deck guns were moved to the superstructure and the upper deck tubes removed. They achieved nothing in World War 1, except an extraordinary and tragic collision that suggests faulty deployment. Of the seventeen built, no fewer than ten all put to sea together in January 1918 and joined up with the Grand Fleet. In pitch darkness K22 found her helm suddenly run hard-over to starboard and jammed. At high speed she veered into K14, hit hard and the vessels locked together. There followed a series of collisions which left K4 and K17 on the bottom, with all hands, and four other K class damaged.

British improved K and X1 (31)

Three even larger submarines intended as K class vessels were eventually completed as the M class. In 1923 a final member of this unhappy series, K26, was completed with a number of modifications. Armed with three 4 in. guns and ten tubes, she was potentially formidable but in fact proved less useful than smaller conventional submarines. But the 'fleet submarine' did rear its head twice more after the development of diesel engines had at last made the steam boiler and its furnaces unnecessary. The first time occurred in the early post-war years, when an impressive submarine of completely new design was produced by Vickers and the Admiralty and built at Chatham. Styled X1 to denote her radical nature, she was completed in 1925. Her main feature, apart from her very powerful diesels, was a pair of large gun turrets each mounting two 5·2 in. guns. She could dive exceptionally deep for her day, and remain submerged 2½ days. She was, in fact, proclaimed to be 'a submersible cruiser'—just as one could almost claim the M class to have been submersible battleships—but accomplished little and was scrapped in 1936. The second revival of the 'fleet submarine' came in the early 1930s with the River class described later.

British M class   (32)

Laid down as four further units of the K class, these vessels were completed to a totally different design. They had diesel engines, and instead of three 4 in. guns were fitted with a monster 12 in. (305 mm) gun in a 60-ton turret. The guns had come from scrapped Majestic class battleships. The intention was that they should be submersible monitors, but the big gun was judged equally useful for use against ships, the shells being cheaper and more numerous than a submarine's torpedoes. M1 was commissioned in 1918, and the next two in 1919 and 1920; M4 was left unfinished. Cdr Horton (p.108) was appointed to M1, took

her to the Mediterranean and might have proved the general principle had it not been for the Armistice.

The idea was to search at 30 ft periscope depth for a target, line up the big vessel exactly (there was no traverse) with the gun at about 45 deg. elevation and rise until about 6 ft of barrel was clear of the water. After firing one round, it then took 55 seconds to submerge again to periscope depth, for reloading. One of the first lessons learned the hard way was that if there was much seawater in the gun barrel it would burst on firing a round. Another basic point was that accuracy was poor, though using the 'dip chick' (point-blank) technique against surface ships was another matter. M1 was then painted green, her sisters being dark grey and dark blue, and used in aerial ASW experiments until she vanished in the English Channel on a windy night in November 1925. Weeks later it was thought that she must have surfaced under the bows of the Swedish collier Vidar, whose hull was heavily marked with dark green paint, which proved to be the identical specification.

M2 was by this time being rebuilt as an aircraft carrier, recommissioning in 1927 with a small watertight hangar in place of the big gun. George Parnall & Co. supplied the small Peto twin-float seaplane, which was catapulted off the surfaced vessel on reconnaissance missions, landed alongside, and was fished aboard by a crane and folded into its hangar. Generally the submarine/aircraft team was technically successful, until on 26 January 1932 M2 was lost with all hands just off Portland; it was widely supposed she had dived with both inner and outer hangar doors open, though the Admiralty never disclosed the cause. This left only M3, which had been converted into by far the most capable of submarine minelayers. She had a huge superstructure casing over her load of more than 100 mines, and apparently suffered no disasters in her subsequent career. She was scrapped in 1939.

British R class (33)

Dating from 1917, this group (R1–10) was the first ever to be designed explicitly to kill hostile submarines. As a result they were planned to be faster underwater than on the surface. They had fat well-rounded bows, a beautifully streamlined hull with slim conning tower, no gun, and tremendous electric battery capacity driving a single screw at the extreme stern. Their underwater speed set a record that was not to be surpassed for 25 years, and then only by research craft. They carried the latest sound-detection equipment, and all six tubes (originally 18 in. but later exchanged for the new 21 in. calibre) were in the bow. One of them successfully tracked a U-boat and fired a torpedo which failed to explode. Had it done so, the R class might have been thought about a little deeper.

Nobody at the time recognised that in these ten submarines were all the features that would characterise the submarines being designed at the end (but not at the beginning) of World War 2. Instead they were regarded as freaks, and were all sold in 1923. While underwater speed and stealth were ignored, the next quarter century saw persistent efforts to make submarines go faster on the surface.

US World War 1 classes

All early US Navy submarines were built to Navy requirements along the basic designs of either Holland or Lake, in small groups each introducing a few improvements. When the United States entered the war in April 1917 the US Navy had twenty-four submarines, all diesel-engined, though they were used sparingly. The first type to play a significant role in the war was the N class of 1916, a typical saddle-tank design with NLSE diesels (German MAN-licence). The slightly larger O class of 1917 was similar, comprising O1–10 of Holland type and O11–16 of Lake type. Then came the much more important R class, which were longer and had the new 21 in. tubes; R1–20 were Hollands and R21–27 were Lakes, all delivered in 1918–19. Up to this point nearly all US submarines had been built at the Fore River yard at Quincy, but now the Union Iron Works at San Francisco, Bethlehem Steel at Quincy and the Portsmouth Navy Yard began deliveries. The Armistice intervened before the big S class could become effective. In

1941 three R class were supplied under Lend-Lease to the Royal Navy, which renumbered them P511, 512 and 514 and used them for training.

US S class

Into this important class went the accumulated experience of all the American submarine designers. Three prototypes were built, S1 being a Holland type, S2 a Lake and S3 being the first designed by the Navy itself (the Bureau of Construction and Repair). The Lake system was finally abandoned, and production comprised S4–17 to the Bureau design and S18–41 of Holland type. These boats were a significant advance in size, power, speed, range and torpedo reload capacity. Later the range was increased further in S42–47 (Holland) and S48–51 (Bureau) which were longer and had larger bunkers. During the 1920s Electric Boat built four similar vessels for Peru. In 1923 S1 carried a small Martin Kitten landplane in a tubular hangar abaft the conning tower. By 1930 three, S4, S5 and S51, had been lost in accidents, and during the 1930s S2, 3, 6–10, 19, 49 and 50 were scrapped. In 1942 six, including S1, were supplied by Lend-Lease to the Royal Navy, which renumbered them P551–56 and used them for training until the end of 1942.

SUBMARINE DEVELOPMENT 1918–45

Few of the victors in World War 1 were emotionally disposed to try to learn much from the vanquished. For several years the emphasis was strongly on rundown and retrenchment, but gradually the navies of the major powers learned to live in an austere financial environment and to go forward once more in opening up the boundaries of submarine possibilities. Several 'freak' submarines were built, either new or as conversions, among them being vessels with 12 in. (305 mm) guns and equally large submarines equipped to launch and retrieve aircraft.

In most countries the inter-war years were ones in which navies were small and professional, and, due to the sluggish rate of introduction of new equipment, most crews were outstandingly skilled and proficient. Despite this the incidence of submarine disasters was high, and experience was bought at a tragically high price. Gradually hull design was improved, propulsion systems improved and rationalised (with almost 100 per cent. adoption of diesel surface propulsion), and rather reluctant attention paid to the design, perfection and introduction of escape apparatus for stricken crews.

Globally, the Washington Treaty was seen by many as a route towards preventing an arms race by artificially limiting the sizes of navies. Only one country, Japan, visibly scorned such a treaty and continued progressive build-up of a formidable navy which was particularly strong in submarines. Like the American submarines, the Japanese ones were generally much larger than those of European nations, reflecting the vast size of the Pacific Ocean. In contrast, the Royal Navy, and to some degree France and Italy, concentrated upon small 'coastal' submarines tailored to the kind of European war the planners foresaw. Britain's brief excursion into the 'fleet submarine' (K class) was abandoned, though in the 1930s three much more practical large high-speed submarines were commissioned (River class) but never used with surface fleets. Several nations built special mine-laying submarines, and a few unconventional experimental vessels were commissioned, but in the main 1919–39 was a period of consolidation along established lines. Especially important was the introduction of all-welded hulls in the United States in 1928–30. This enabled submarines to dive deeper and stand up better to depth-charge attack.

Technically the period was noted for two major developments, beside which all the giant submarine monsters were aberrations. In the field of submarines the development of a long telescopic pipe enabling diesel engines to run at periscope depth was an obvious idea but was never carried to fruition until the Dutch O21 class of 1937. Amazingly, when O21–24 escaped to Britain in 1940 the Royal Navy took away their newfangled 'air masts', and it was not until 1943 that the Germans realised the importance of the pipes they had found in the Rotterdam yard (and, as the world knows, named it the Schnorkel, shortened in English to snort). The other development was Asdic (and later sonar), which by the mid-1930s had become the main way the Royal Navy searched for submerged submarines. Curiously, while underwater detection made significant progress, little was done to improve anti-submarine weapons.

World War 2 submarines were almost all merely improved versions of classes developed during the previous two decades. There were only two completely new wartime developments. One was the fairly widespread use of extremely small 'midget' submarines, even smaller re-usable 'human torpedoes' for attaching charges to enemy hulls, and—by the Germans and Japanese as a final desperate measure—true human torpedoes which made a one-way trip. The other was the early recognition by Germany that something had to be done to provide much greater underwater propulsive power. Concentrated hydrogen peroxide used to fuel steam turbines was one answer, but a better one was just to instal far greater electric battery capacity and more powerful motors.

French large submarines (34/35)

Pride of place must be given to the submarine Surcouf, one of the most famous ever built. In her day she was easily the biggest and heaviest submarine, and also included in her armament two 203 mm (8 in.) guns and a spotter aircraft. Whether or not she was sensible is arguable, but the reason for her existence seems to have been the clause in the Washington Naval Treaty stipulating that submarines must not carry guns larger than 8 in. Authorised in 1925 and laid down in 1927, she finally commissioned in 1934 and then spent years being modified and refitted before finally working up to operational trim. By 1939 she was fully battleworthy, and in June 1940 she chose to escape from a refit at Brest to Britain. This was a refreshing contrast to most of the French fleet, which for the rest of World War 2 was in the main fighting against the Allies in North Africa, the Mediterranean, Syria and Indo-China, and ended up

either wrecked by Allied fire, scuttled or in enemy hands. Not so the Surcouf, which was eventually again made ready for sea and, in the hands of an FNFL (Free French Navy) crew, operated gallantly in the Atlantic and Caribbean. It was an unfortunate accident that, on 18 February 1942, she was run down by an American freighter in the Gulf of Mexico.

The first submarines ordered in France after World War 1 were the Requin class, of which nine were completed in 1926–27. Refitted in 1936–37, all operated in World War 2 until the French capitulation on 25 June. Only one, Narval, joined the Allies in Malta; the rest were eventually sunk by Allied forces or scuttled. The very large Redoutable class of thirty-one boats were considerably bigger, and had much greater range. They also introduced the 400 mm (15·75 in.) torpedo, which was a short-ranged weapon for use against merchant ships— and an abject failure. Even the big 550 mm (21·7 in.) torpedo was inaccurate except on a straight run. The French persisted in trainable deck tubes, in both calibres, for surface attack. Two Redoutables were lost in the 1930s and one was torpedoed by a U-boat; of the rest, only one, Casablanca, assisted the Allied cause, the remainder being scuttled, scrapped or destroyed fighting Allied forces.

French smaller submarines (36)

Many small groups of 600-ton submarines were built in the inter-war years, in three main families Loire/Simonot, Schneider/Laubeuf and Normand/Fenaux. Altogether thirty-five were in existence at the start of World War 2; one was soon sunk, and of the others two fought for the Allies (Junon and Minerve), performing many difficult and dangerous missions. The final French classes were uncompleted, except for the excellent small minelayers of the Saphir type. Six of these were completed in 1930-37, with the Normand/Fenaux system derived from the British E class of 1915. Two mines were fitted into each of sixteen vertical tubes arranged along the lateral ballast tanks, and the system worked well (using Vickers mines because of failure of supply of the French pattern). Two of the six boats joined the Allies. Perle operated in several theatres until she was tragically sunk in error by a British aircraft soon after D-day. Rubis performed twenty-two courageous sorties laying mines and torpedoing enemy vessels, and survived the war.

British O, P, R, Porpoise classes (37)

Having failed to get submarines outlawed at the 1921 Washington Conference, it was logical to use the L class as the basis for the Royal Navy's first post-war patrol submarines. Laid down at Barrow in 1925, the first units of the O class (for the Royal Australian Navy) revealed a considerable increase in beam and bunker capacity compared with the L ships, and this was used not only to extend range but also in doubling the number of tubes and improving interior appointments and space. One of their few faults was that oil leaked from their riveted exterior saddle tanks, leaving a tell-tale slick on the surface. Type 118 Asdic was standard at first, and the hydrophone was at last abandoned. Nine were built: Oberon, Otway, Oxley, Odin, Olympus, Orpheus, Osiris, Oswald and Otus. By 1942 the survivors were taken off operations and used for training.

Generally similar, the P and R classes were slightly larger, had a flared bow and larger conning tower with the gun almost level with the top: Parthian, Perseus, Phoenix, Poseidon, Pandora, Proteus, Rainbow, Regent, Rover, Regulus. Poseidon was tragically lost in an exercise in 1931, and both classes were almost wiped out in World War 2.

Slightly slimmer, but with greater displacement, the Porpoise class affirmed the Admiralty's belief that minelaying warranted a purpose-designed vessel. Designed in 1933, these ships—Porpoise, Grampus, Narwhal, Cachalot, Rorqual and Seal—each carried fifty mines, strewn through stern doors. The last of the class, Seal, was captured as a wreck in the Kattegat on 5 May 1940, taken into German service as UA and finally scrapped in 1941.

British River class (38)
During the 1920s the big high-performance X1 'submersible cruiser' kept the idea of a 'fleet submarine' simmering, and with the continued improvement of marine diesel engines the Admiralty decided in 1927 to authorise three new large submarines with high surface speed. These were quite conventional vessels, without any large guns or other unusual features, and they were long and relatively well streamlined for their day. After being launched in 1932 the first of the trio was christened Thames, one of the first British submarines to bear a name. Her sisters were the slightly larger Severn and Clyde. All three served in World War 2. They were certainly successful, but perhaps did little more than other British submarines of the same period that cost half as much to build and operate (with the single exception of a vital cargo mission to Malta in September 1941 by Clyde, carrying no less than 1,200 tons of desperately needed stores). They were the last high-speed diesel boats that attempted to match the surface speed of surface vessels. It was soon realised that it is under-water speed that matters.

US V class
During the 1920s the US Navy had more S class submarines than it had funds to operate, and the last thing it wanted was to buy new submarines. But after 1925 the evident need for improved designs eventually forced small submarine-building appropriations out of Congress, and the Navy yards designed and built eight large new long-range submarines known as the V class. They had air-conditioned interiors more spacious and much better arranged than the S class, their performance was slightly better and they carried considerably more oil fuel and had greater range than almost any previous production submarines.

The main reason for this was the realisation that Japan was becoming more of a threat than Europe, and that the distances in the Pacific were enormous. Having designs based on the German UA cruisers, and the big American T1–3 of 1919–20, the first three (V1–3) were launched in 1924–25 and named Barracuda, Bass and Bonita. By earlier standards they were enormous, with double hulls and two sets of diesel engines, one driving the screws and the other the generators. There followed the monster V4 Argonaut of 1927, and then Narwhal and Nautilus of 1929–30, all huge vessels with two 6 in. guns and either a mass of torpedoes or (V4) mines. V7 Dolphin was an attempt to get the same fighting power in a vessel of half the displacement, the only real reduction in power being loss of the big guns.

In 1931 the Navy decided to allow private yards to tender for additional submarines of this general type, partly to alleviate the depression. Not unexpectedly the ninth boat was awarded to Electric Boat, at Groton, which had managed to eke out a living since 1918 on odd jobs and the manufacture of the batch of S class submarines for Peru. In view of the company's experience EB was allowed to modify the design, and the resulting boat, USS Cuttlefish, was smaller and improved in detail, like her Navy-built sister V8 Cachalot. Her best feature was her double hull, of mainly welded construction, in which she broke important new ground. Launched in November 1933 Cuttlefish was not only the first of six similar US Navy contracts placed during the 1930s but also the most important stepping-stone to the outstanding submarines of World War 2. The US Navy could easily have concentrated on short-range designs for coastal defence. It was rather fortuitous that, partly as a result of technology pioneered at Groton during the 1930s, by 1941 the US Navy had the capability and proven designs for rapid production of the longest-ranged submarines in the world, with outstanding all-round fighting qualities.

US Porpoise class

Though dwarfed in importance by the Gato and Balao classes that were standard in World War 2, these ten boats firmly set the style that was to be followed. They were of around 1,500 tons, carried 373 tons of oil fuel and were well equipped for operation anywhere in the world. The 1930 London Naval Treaty had imposed a severe limit on US submarine tonnage, and everything possible was done with this class to reduce weight, one major factor being the decision to use high-speed (over 700 rpm) diesel engines. A choice of four makes was available—Winton, General Motors, HOR and Fairbanks Morse—and all were selected in 1933 for prototype submarines, three of them in this class. As noise was not at this time appreciated as of potential importance in submarines, each of the two screws was driven by two geared diesels and two geared electric motors. The class comprised three groups: Porpoise and Pike, with 3 in. gun; Shark, Tarpon, with 4 in. gun; and Perch, Pickerel, Permit, Plunger, Pollack and Pompano, with longer hull, different engines and, in the first three, two extra reload torpedoes.

US Salmon and Sargo classes

Slightly larger than the final Porpoise boats, these were close to the optimum design for the US Navy missions, having immense range and excellent performance within a modest size (though very large in comparison with most European submarines). Their torpedo armament was especially powerful, and they were almost as fast on the surface as the generally similar Japanese I74 series with almost double the diesel power. There were two groups, closely similar except that in the first (Salmon, Seal, Skipjack, Snapper, Stingray and Sturgeon) each shaft was driven by one diesel and two electric motors, with other diesels driving the generators, while the second group (Sargo, Saury, Spearfish, Sculpin, Squalus [later renamed Sailfish], Swordfish, Seadragon, Sealion, Searaven and Seawolf) had ordinary geared diesel/electric drive with one large motor on each shaft. Like all other US submarines, these were considerably refitted in 1941–42, being equipped with radar, augmented AA armament of 20 mm or 40 mm guns and various other detail changes to improve fighting efficiency.

US Tambor and Gar classes
Generally similar to the preceding vessels, these had direct-drive propulsion. The noise and weight were reduced, but as two diesels were needed on each shaft difficulties were experienced in sharing the work (rear engines bore most of the load), and propulsion power dropped by half when batteries were being recharged. The first group had GM engines and 374-ton bunkers (Tambor, Tautog, Thresher, Triton, Trout and Tuna). The second had Fairbanks Morse engines and 385-ton bunkers (Gar, Grampus, Grayback, Grayling, Grenadier and Gudgeon).

US Gato class (39)
Steady development between the wars had brought the US submarine to a fine pitch when Gato,

lead-ship of the biggest class of boats then ordered, slid down the ways at Groton in August 1941. The problem of propulsion was settled, undoubtedly wisely, by using two pairs of high-speed diesels to drive generators which supplied a geared electric motor on each shaft. As in earlier US submarines the interior was fully air-conditioned and, by comparison with a U-boat, palatial, with bunks in one room and a mess in another (in a U-VIIC both functions were served by the fore torpedo room), and numerous conveniences not found in other navies. As in earlier classes the Gato boats were modified after 1941 to have different gun armament (the 3 in. gun abaft the conning tower was often moved forward, or replaced by a 4 in. or 5 in.) and much augmented AA defence (the 0·30 in. Browning being supplemented by 0·50 in., 20 mm singles and twins and sometimes a 40 mm), while every Gato submarine was soon being equipped with increasing radar, countermeasures and new communications. The welded hull facilitated mass production on a prefabricated basis, and during the first half of 1942 three new yards were opened, while existing facilities were expanded; Electric Boat, for example, increased its number of submarine slipways from three to thirteen.

Though there were differences in diesel and electric suppliers, and in bunker capacity, the following can be treated as one class: Gato, Greenling, Grouper, Growler, Grunion, Guardfish, Albacore, Amberjack, Barb, Blackfish, Bluefish, Bonefish, Cod, Cero, Corvina, Darter, Drum, Flying Fish, Finback, Haddock, Halibut, Herring, Kingfish, Shad, Silversides, Trigger, Wahoo, Whale, Angler, Bashaw, Bluegill, Bream, Cavalla, Cobia, Croaker, Dace, Dorado, Flasher, Flier, Flounder, Gabilan, Gunnel, Gurnard, Haddo, Hake, Harder, Hoe, Jack, Lapon, Mingo, Muskallunge, Paddle, Pargo, Peto, Pogy, Pompon, Puffer, Rasher, Raton, Ray, Redfin, Robalo, Rock, Runner, Sawfish, Scamp, Scorpion, Snook, Steelhead, Sunfish, Tunny, Tinosa and Tullibee. Many of the war losses incurred were never explained; some boats just failed to return, Dorado was bombed by American aircraft in error, and Tullibee was hit by a faulty torpedo she herself had fired!

US Balao class (40/41)

This great class, the biggest of any Allied type of submarine, was almost identical to the Gato type. All had at least 464 tons of fuel and most had 472; and all had a 5 in. gun, the most common final gun arrangement being a 5 in. on the foredeck, a 40 mm AA on the front of the conning tower and a 20 mm aft. A few, such as the radar picket Blueback, had two 5 in. and two 40 mm. The hull was strengthened for diving to 400 ft, 100 ft deeper than the Gato class. Names were: Balao, Billfish, Bowfin, Cabrilla, Capelin, Cisco, Crevalle, Devilfish, Dragonet, Escolar, Hackleback, Lancetfish, Ling, Lionfish, Manta, Moray, Roncador, Sabalo, Sablefish

Seahorse, Skate, Tang, Tilefish, Apagon, Aspro, Batfish, Archerfish, Burrfish, Perch, Shark, Sealion, Barbel, Barbero, Baya, Becuna, Bergall, Besugo, Blackfin, Caiman, Blenny, Blower, Blueback, Boarfish, Charr, Chub, Brill, Bugara, Bullhead, Bumper, Cabezon, Dentuda, Capitaine, Carbonero, Carp, Catfish, Entemedor, Chivo, Chopper, Clamagore, Cobbler, Cochino, Corporal, Cubera, Cusk, Diodon, Dogfish, Greenfish, Halfbeak, Golet, Guavina, Guitarro, Hammerhead, Hardhead, Hawkbill, Icefish, Jallao, Kete, Kraken, Lagarto, Lamprey, Lizardfish, Loggerhead, Macabi, Mapiro, Menhaden, Mero, Sand Lance, Picuda, Pampanito, Parche, Bang, Pilotfish, Pintado, Pipefish, Piranha, Plaice, Pomfret, Sterlet, Queenfish, Razorback, Redfish, Ronquil, Scabbardfish, Segundo, Sea Cat, Sea Devil, Sea Dog, Sea Fox, Atule, Spikefish, Sea Owl, Sea Poacher, Sea Robin, Sennet, Piper, Threadfin, Spadefish, Trepang, Spot, Springer, Stickleback and Tiru.

By the time these boats entered service the serious fault of American torpedoes to run under their targets, in 1940-42, had been overcome. The universal fitment of radar was of great benefit, because in the Pacific these large submarines operated normally on the surface where they needed both to find targets at night or in bad weather and also to have warning of enemy aircraft, and, expecially, of the presence of hostile radars. The best assessment of these boats and their crews is the average of 50,000 tons of

Japanese shipping sunk each month by submarines in 1943, rising to no less than 200,000-plus tons per month in the first 6 months of 1944. After July 1944 the tonnage fell, because there were very few Japanese ships left to sink. More than any other single factor—say many strategists—Japan was defeated by her complete isolation resulting from the destruction of her shipping.

As for results against Japanese warships, US submarines sank 214 ships in all including one battleship, eight carriers, fifteen cruisers, forty-two destroyers and twenty-three submarines, for the loss of fifty-two of their own number. By 1944 it was not unusual for US submarines to sink more anti-submarine escorts than the number of submarines sunk by those forces. The degree of competence and nerve required can be judged from the fact that the common technique was to steer at the oncoming enemy vessel and, at the last moment, release a fan of torpedoes in the so-called 'down the throat' shot. The Japanese steadfastly refused to adopt the convoy system, and with the down-the-throat shot the hunters became the hunted.

US Tench class (41/68)

Again based on the Gato, this would have been the biggest class of all had the war continued. In the event thirty-three were completed, at the end of the war, and 101 were cancelled. All had a 5 in. gun aft, and many had a second for'ard; there were various arrangements of 20

mm and 40 mm AA guns. Vessels completed were: Tusk, Corsair, Argonaut, Runner, Conger, Cutlass, Diabolo, Medregal, Requin, Irex, Sea Leopard, Odax, Sirago, Pomodon, Remora, Sarda, Spinax, Volador, Amberjack, Pickerel, Grenadier, Tigrone, Grampus, Trumpetfish, Unicorn, Walrus, Quillback, Tench, Thornback, Tirante, Toro and Torsk. These were the last wartime builds. The next class, never built, would have been longer and more powerful, with six 12 in. AS torpedo tubes firing to each beam.

Japanese submarines

Between the World Wars Japanese submarine development was technically interesting and often impressive, but the result was a hotch-potch of small classes and individual 'one-off' vessels mostly conceived with the idea that submarines operated as part of a surface fleet. The first indigenous boat was a very large and fast long-range submarine which could outperform any previously built (except in the matter of surface speed, when the British K class could just beat it). Designated No 44 at first, and later redesignated I51, it was also called Type KD1; Japanese submarine designations defied any easy classification or arrangement.

Subsequent vessels were smaller and usually slower, and in the four RO29 boats sank to 665 tons and 13 knots, with a range of 6,900 miles, hardly adequate for Pacific operations. Nine were built to the Type

L4 design, derived from the British L class and powered by Vickers diesels, and numbered RO60-68. In the mid-1920s came the four big J1 (Junsen) type, numbered I1-4, all of which operated in World War 2, ultimately as transports in which role they were wiped out. There were also nine very similar KD3A and KD3B boats, numbered I53-60 and 63 (from 1938-42 all survivors of early classes had their numbers increased by 100, so that these became I153-159, the final two having been lost). Several further 'one-offs' and small groups led in 1933-36 to the KD6A type, numbered I68-73 (later I168-172, the last having been sunk). These six wrought much havoc, by far the biggest victim being the carrier Yorktown; all were sunk. Further steps led to Type C1 of 1938-40, numbered 16, 18, 20, 22 and 24. These were bigger and faster KD6As, with a 16,100-mile radius of action. Like many of the larger classes they later carried midget submarines, and all were sunk. Biggest and most important pre-war class was Type B1, numbered I15, 17, 19, 21, 32 and 25-39. These twenty large vessels were delivered in 1939-43, and not only had a 5·5 in. gun and twin 25 mm AA guns but also a small reconnaissance seaplane in a surprisingly small hangar faired into the conning tower. In World War 2 they sank many ships from the carrier Wasp down, but all were destroyed before the end of 1944 save I36, which survived as a near total-loss (she was then scuttled).

Japanese World War 2 classes (42)

The first class of submarines delivered during World War 2 in Japan was Type KS, numbered RO100-117. These small coastal boats were low in speed and range, yet were consistently used against heavily defended fleets; all were sunk. There followed the Type KD7 (I176-185), which were larger and much faster yet accomplished little and were likewise wiped out. Only one example survived of the Type K6 class of medium (960-ton) vessels delivered in 1942-44, which for the loss of seventeen of their own number (RO35-49, 55 and 56) sank one destroyer escort and one landing craft. There were three of the big Type C2, numbered I46-48, and three C3 (I52-53 and 55) and B3 (I54, 56, 58), all of over 2,000 tons and carrying one or two 5·5 in. guns and eventually serving as carriers for Kaiten suicide boats. There were only two in each of the next two classes of large boats (SH, numbered I351-352, and AM, numbered I1 and 13). Many of all these classes were cancelled, because clearly the Imperial submarines were being wiped out and little was being accomplished. The Type D1 class, however, was continued from I361-372, because these smaller boats were desperately needed to carry supplies to beleaguered island garrisons. All save one were sunk, and none sank any enemy vessels (they had guns only, and tried to keep out of the enemy's way). Likewise, most of the big D2s were cancelled, and only I373-

4 were completed as transports, without tubes.

Technically the Type STo, ordered in 1942 and larger than any previous submarines, surpassed anything else of the period; but again they were a total dead loss. Admiral Yamamoto was anxious to stop construction of existing submarines of large and medium types, and to concentrate on very small and suicide designs and on huge monsters that were almost a navy in themselves. The STo carried heavy armament of all kinds, as well as a hangar for three bomber aircraft which were intended to have no landing gear and be recovered after ditching alongside. Two types of aircraft were developed: the Aichi M6A Seiran, a high-performance attacker which actually finished up with twin seaplane floats, and the Yokosuka E14Y, a light reconnaissance machine. These huge submarines had hulls with two pressure lobes side by side like a flat figure 8. The hangar was offset to starboard and the conning tower to port, and the long catapult extended almost to the bows. Though their diving depth of 100 m. (328 ft) was poor compared with European boats, it was distinctly deeper than any other Japanese submarine, and their patrol endurance of 90 days and radius of action of 43,200 miles handsomely exceeded anything that could be attained by any other submarine in the pre-nuclear era. The only examples completed were I400–402, the last being converted into a tanker. No others were completed

though 404 was sunk by bombs while unfinished at the Kure yard.

There were no more conventional Japanese submarines, and the story so far is a catalogue of disasters, due almost entirely to supremely misguided management and operational deployment. But in 1938 a research submarine of under 200 tons had achieved the amazing underwater speed of $21\frac{1}{4}$ knots, as a result of having better streamlining and much greater electrical capacity and motor power. This paved the way for two classes of small submarine which, had they followed on close behind the experimental craft, might have been important. The first class was Type ST, a remarkable technical achievement with a beautifully streamlined hull and fin-like tower, and a deck gun that folded away and was covered by doors. Welded prefabricated construction promised a high rate of output, and the all-round performance of these boats was fantastic, surpassing even the German Type XXI. None became operational, however, and of I201–223 only the first nine were started and four completed. But in 1945 the Japanese launched a crash programme for a small, cheap, mass-produced defensive submarine to protect the homeland, rather like the Heinkel 162 'People's Fighter' aircraft urgently produced in Germany. The Type STS, numbered from Ha201 onwards, was a remarkable design which for cost/effectiveness has possibly never been rivalled. It was really a miniature ST, scaled down to 320 tons. Their big battery power gave them a fair submerged speed of 13 knots, and they actually had snorts and radar, and like the ST class could dive to more than 100 m. (328 ft). Starting in March 1945 it was hoped to turn out ninety very quickly, but in fact only ten were complete at the surrender and none was ready for action.

Japanese suicide craft (43/45)

The first move in the direction of a 'human torpedo' came with the construction of two midget submarines in 1943. Based on the Type A, they had lateral diving planes and other changes, and a crew of one. In the following year tests began on a batch of a smaller model having a slim torpedo-shaped hull, which served as the prototype of the Kairyu, ordered in large numbers from nine yards (eight of them uncommitted to Koryu production) in late 1944. As a typical last-ditch programme, there was no proper planning, and Kairyus were built with different kinds of armament, equipment and engine. Most had a standard auto engine with electric underwater propulsion giving only a modest speed. The intention was to arm the Kairyu with two torpedoes, released individually from external crutches, but the unavailability of torpedoes caused production to standardise on the suicide version with a 1,320 lb warhead. Like the Koryu, some Kairyus were fitted with a larger conning tower and dual periscopes and used to train suicide volunteers, but most of those discovered at the

surrender were suicide craft. At least 207 completed examples were found at Yokosuka alone, which was the centre of Kairyu development, but there is no record of operational use.

Far better known was the Kaiten series, which were truly manned torpedoes. Throughout the war the only aspect of Japanese naval hardware that was better than that of the Allies was the superb Type 93 Long Lance torpedo, with calibre of 600 mm (23·62 in.) and a devastating 3,418 lb warhead. It was powered by a unique engine burning petrol and stored gaseous oxygen, developing about 550 h.p. This propulsion system was used to drive the first Kaiten 1 series, which had fatter and much longer bodies and a seat for an operator behind the warhead under a transparent Plexiglas dome. Some of the first models had a hatch on the underside intended to allow the operator to escape during the last run-in to the target, but such escape would appear very difficult to accomplish; in any case the hatch was soon deleted. Operation was again an improperly developed procedure. Kaitens were launched from a catapulted cradle from surface vessels rather in the way mines were sown over the stern. It was the task of the operator to set course for the enemy vessel, running underwater most of the time but doing his best to snatch periodic glimpses of the target by direct vision through the cupola. Steering was entirely by his commands, there being no gyropilot or homing device. Absence of a periscope would appear to have posed problems, though there are few records of development trials. Production began at the beginning of 1945, at the rate of several hundred per month. All submarines then under construction, except for the ST and STS types, were scrapped in the yards to make way for midgets and suicide craft. By 1945 the whole emphasis was on Kaitens, but by this time there were severe shortages which led to uncompleted Kaitens being used as fuel tanks on supply submarines.

Many of these discarded hulls were intended for the larger Kaiten 2, 3 and 4 models, which had much greater power, speed and range, and usually needed a crew of two. Kaiten 2 introduced the new 1,500 h.p. No 6 engine developed with German Walter technology and running on Perhydrol (concentrated hydrogen peroxide). This would have proved ideal if it had been properly developed, but the Japanese were unable to make more than a handful of these engines. The Kaiten 3 never got into production at all, and only a handful of Kaiten 45 were built with a 1,500 h.p. petrol/oxygen propulsion system. Operationally the main carriers for Kaitens were to be the surviving large submarines, all of which were intended to be recalled and modified as Kaiten launchers. Conversion began as early as December 1944, with provision for four Kaitens on deck, released by the diving of the parent submarine. By March 1945 the number carried was increased where possible to six, two

on the foredeck and six alongside the conning tower and to the rear. There was no shortage of Kaiten crews, and the most remarkable thing about this large-scale effort is the lack of results it achieved.

Japanese midgets (44/45)

Attention to a midget submarine was first given by Kure Navy Yard in 1934. After three steps in development, production began on the Type A vessel in 1938. At first the superimposed bow tubes were open at the front, but by the time five from the Imperial 6th Fleet had tried (unsuccessfully) to penetrate Pearl Harbor on 7 December 1941 the front holes had caps and protection against nets, with jumping wires over the central conning tower. The Type A achieved little but public alarm on a mission against Sydney Harbour in 1942, but later in that year one succeeded in torpedoing the old British battleship Ramillies anchored at Diego Suarez during the occupation of Madagascar. About sixty were built.

Further experiments with the Type B midget, with a diesel generator for recharging the batteries, led to fifteen of the Type C. This was rather larger than Type A, and had a crew of three and vastly increased radius of action. Finally, in January 1945, the prototype was completed of the Koryu (Midget) Type D, which was a really formidable boat, though not quite so fast underwater as the speedy A and C. With a crew of five, this had a much more powerful diesel and radius of action of 1,115 miles. Many hundreds were ordered from twelve yards, the initial programme being 180 per month with deliveries from September 1945. The prefabricated sections were small enough to be transported by ordinary trucks, and various modifications were made to speed production. This was not so much a true midget as a very small submarine, because it had a crew of five with bunks and provisions. Small numbers were used in the defence of Okinawa and the Philippines, and several were discovered with large suicide warheads (probably because of the extreme shortage of torpedoes). Total completions were not much more than 100, the actual total being hard to determine because of the chaotic state of the Japanese yards. More than 40 were found at the Kure yard alone, but production at this great yard had long since come to a halt through various crippling shortages.

Italian medium submarines (46/47)

There was considerable standardisation and large numbers of each type. Especially was this the case with the Sirena, Perla, Adua and Acciaio classes, all of which were closely similar and formed a group of fifty-two submarines which saw more action than most Italian naval construction. Perla, name-ship of her class, was one of those based at Bordeaux after Italy's entry to the war in June 1940, operating in the Atlantic from May 1941. She returned to the Mediterranean, and on 9 July 1942 was captured by a British corvette and eventually

commissioned as HM Submarine P712. After the war she became the Greek Matrozos. Several other members of this group had eventful careers, Bronzo becoming HM Submarine P714 and then the French submarine Narval. The majority, however, were sunk or scuttled.

Italian large submarines (48)

Between the World Wars it was quite normal for Italian submarine classes to comprise no more than two to four boats, so, though the total force was greater than that of any other naval power, there was no important standard class of vessel. One of the most significant types was the Balilla group of four large submarines completed in 1928–29, which were capable vessels, developed further with the Ettore Fieramosca to carry a small reconnaissance aircraft (never actually provided). Another interesting large type was the R class, designed purely as transports and carrying no armament other than three 20 mm AA guns; they had holds for 610 tons of urgent cargo, but nearly all of this class of twelve was scuttled or destroyed on the slipway in the manner that became the fate of most Italian submarines in World War 2. Only a very small proportion of the Italian force of large boats ever operated, and they did little.

Italian midgets

In addition to two CM class small submarines, the Italians developed several species of midget submarine earlier than other nations. The CA class of four boats (two with diesel/electric propulsion and two with batteries only) had a crew of three and was designed in 1935–36 to launch two torpedoes. As completed in 1937–43, they carried instead eight demolition charges of 220 lb each, sometimes augmented by a group of smaller charges. None accomplished anything, but the CB class of twenty-two did see some action, CB1–6 being transferred to Roumania for use in the Black Sea (where CB5 was torpedoed by a Soviet aircraft).

Italian SLC (human torpedo) (49)

In sharp contrast to the almost entirely negative record of Italian submarines, these 'human torpedoes' were technically in advance of their time, demanded immense courage on the part of their crews, and established a fine record of war operation. Drawing partly on experience gained with various kinds of harbour assault in World War 1, the SLC (Siluro a Lenta Corsa, slow-course torpedo) was designed at a mansion near La Spezia about 1936, and developed at San Bartolomeo torpedo works. It resembled a fat torpedo on which two men could ride, protected by a simple superstructure. They wore protective clothing of the kind which much later was given the name of a Frogman's outfit, while they had backpacks of the kind later called SCUBA (self-contained underwater breathing apparatus). Propulsion

was by a low-power, almost silent electric motor. Hopefully the device would be able to penetrate enemy harbours or anchored shipping and allow the operators to attach the large explosive charge carried on the SLC's nose. At first the charge was of 485 lb, but it later grew to 551 lb and finally to 661 lb.

As the range was less than 15 miles, the SLC was to be carried to the scene of action by a large submarine equipped to carry three on deck in watertight containers. The Gondar and Sciré were thus converted as SLC carriers in 1939–40, and training began with what had become commonly known as Il Maiale, the Pig. In September 1941 a mission was mounted against Gibraltar with poor results, but an operation against Alexandria on 18 December provided a totally unexpected contrast. Three Maiali managed to slip in behind a British cruiser, with the six black heads of the operators just clear of the water and silently moving at 3 knots. Charges were fixed to the battleships Queen Elizabeth, and Valiant, and to a fleet oiler. All detonated next morning (with the captured frogmen on board the battleships), immobolising the last two Allied capital ships in the Mediterranean.

German Types I and II (50/51)

Forbidden to build or possess submarines by the Versailles Treaty of 1919, Germany sent design teams to Spain, the Netherlands and Soviet Union (the last group moved to Finland) from the mid-1920s to keep in being a nucleus of submarine expertise. In 1927 the first actual design work began, and the first submarine to be built was the Vesikko, launched in Finland under cover of a 'front' company and tested by Germans in civilian clothes in 1931. This 250-ton boat had three tubes in the new standard calibre of 530 mm (21 in.), and a crew of sixteen, and was based on the UB II of 1915. Purchased by the Finns in 1936, she rammed and sank a Soviet submarine in 1939. A larger submarine, E1 of 750 tons, was constructed by a pseudo-Dutch firm in Cadiz (Spain) in 1932, using many parts made in the Netherlands. After trials this was sold to Spain, and then sold again to Turkey as the Gür. Plans of the E1 were also supplied to the Soviet Union. A similar boat built in Finland in 1931–34 was the Vetehinen.

Out of Vesikko evolved the Type IA, the first submarines built by Hitler's Nazi government in defiance of the Versailles Treaty in 1935. Only two were built (U25, U26) and these were soon used only for training. The first operational design was the Type IIA (U1–6), a coastal type which again was relegated to training by 1939. Type IIB (U7–24, U120, U121) had the same engines but was longer-ranged because of larger bunker capacity. By 1940 these had one or two 20 mm AA guns. Type IIC (U56–63) had greater electric battery capacity and still larger oil-fuel bunkers. The coastal type reached its final development with Type IID of 1940 (U137–152), in

which saddle tanks were added to extend the range to 6,500 miles.

German Type VII (52/53)

Though the Admiralty in London must have known about the lone boat that became the Gür, they were spared the knowledge that it would lead to a horde of U-boats far worse than anything suffered by the Allies in World War 1; no fewer than 721 seagoing Type VII boats were built, and in 1941–43 they came close to bringing Germany's main western enemy, Britain, to her knees. Never before or since have so many submarines been built to a similar basic design; yet even this formidable total was too little and too late in comparison with what would have been achieved if Hitler had not consistently ignored the arguments of his Admirals Raeder and, especially, Doenitz, who pressed for Type VII submarines by the hundred back in the 1930s.

As noted earlier, Vetehinen was built in Finland in the early 1930s, derived in turn from UB III of 1917. This also contributed to the basic E1 (Gür) design in planning the first production boats of Type VIIA (U27–36) of 1936. These were the smallest seagoing boats that could be designed, the idea being that more could be built under the London Naval Treaty (for Hitler was anxious to preserve an outward show of abiding by international law). The VIIA proved to be most successful. U32 was operated in anger in the Spanish Civil War, and was adopted as the standard mass-produced type. It was conventional, compact, cheap and simple to build, easy to handle at all times, and extremely reliable. Its chief faults were a somewhat limited range—initially a mere 6,500 miles—and a crowded interior which made conditions for the crew almost inhumanly vile. By 1937 production had switched to the VIIB (U45–55, 73–76, 83–87 and 99–102), a total of twenty-four. These were slightly larger, had saddle tanks, better seaworthiness, more powerful diesels and greater bunker capacity. The VIIB was thought to be the 'ultimate' submarine, but by 1940 it had been superseded by the VIIC, of which 616 were built (U69–72, 77–82, 88–98, 132–136, 201–212, 221–232, 235–329, 331–458, 465–486, 551–683, 701–722, 731–779, 821–822, 825–828, 901–908, 921–930, 951–1032, 1051–1058, 1063–1065). Among many detail changes the VIIC had two externally stowed torpedo reloads and various arrangements of augmented AA armament.

From May 1943 all Type VII submarines were urgently being refitted, the most valuable changes being the fitting of a snort air pipe for charging the batteries whilst submerged, and the extension of the conning tower to have first a pair of 20 mm AA guns, then two such pairs and finally two pairs and one quad—eight heavy fast-firing cannon, supplied with ammunition brought up through watertight tubes in the superstructure deck. By this time life was a desperate battle against aircraft and surface vessels equipped with ever-improving radar, Asdic and sonar, and the submarines had to respond as best they could. The sixty-one VIIC 41/42 boats (U1101–1110, 1131–1132, 1161–1172, 1191–1210, 1271–1279, 1301–1308) had a strengthened hull for diving to a depth of 820 ft, and incorporated augmented AA armament (typically one 37 mm and two pairs of 20 mm) from the start. They also had armoured conning towers, as did most other VIICs by modification. All the VIIC42 boats, a further model, were cancelled so these were the last of this huge class to be built, entirely by prefabricated sections made at countless inland locations and hurriedly assembled at many yards.

There were also a few minelaying Type VIID (U213–218), with a 32 ft section added abaft the conning tower equipped with five free-flood vertical tubes each housing three mines. The extra section also greatly enlarged the bunkers to 199 tons. A transport development was the VIIF (U1059–1062), in which the mine compartment was used to carry twenty-five torpedoes. These also had the 199-ton bunkers, and were the first U-boats used for the resupply of others far out on patrol.

Exploits of the vast fleets of Type VII boats are legion. The sinking of the children's evacuation liner Athenia on the first day of the war was an error of recognition by the commander of U30, but on 17 September 1939, U29 sank the carrier Courageous, and on 14 October Gunther Prien took U47 into the supposedly impenetrable Scapa Flow and sank the battleship Royal Oak. In April 1940 Otto Kretschmer took command of U99, and by the time U99 was sunk by HMS Walker in March 1941 it had sunk more than 300,000 tons of Allied shipping in unrestricted warfare. Prien and another 'ace', Schepke, were also lost in March 1941, following a bag of a further 500,000 tons between them. In October and November 1941 Raeder sent twenty Type VIIs to the Mediterranean; on 13 November U81 sank the carrier Ark Royal and on 25 November U331 blew up the battleship Barham. Malta became almost totally cut off, so that for a time vital supplies had to be sent by isolated British submarines. In June 1942 U372 sank Malta's submarine depot ship, HMS Medway. Meanwhile the mighty Battle of the Atlantic was reaching a crescendo. On 7 December 1941 the United States entered the war, and the U-boats had a field day along the unprotected East Coast, and then moved to the Caribbean, raising sinkings from 4·3 million tons in 1941 to well over 6 million in 1942. By the end of 1942 the U-boat Wolf Packs were no longer the ruthless victors but were being hunted by thousands of sonars and radars from the sea and sky. In April 1943 came the frightful climax: over 600,000 tons of ships were sunk, but with the loss of most of the U-boats on patrol. Doenitz reached out for final victory and found instead defeat.

On 24 May 1943 he recalled his packs. Never again were they a major threat to the Allies.

German Type IX

Standard large ocean-going submarines of the Nazi Kriegsmarine, the Type IX stemmed from the UE II class of 1918. Though considerably larger than the VII family they were not better sea boats, and in any heavy sea the conning tower was often drenched. They were also less manoeuvrable, and played little part in the violent actions in the North Atlantic and near Europe, instead roaming the Indian Ocean and Pacific. On such long missions they began packed with stores, so that though ostensibly they offered interior accommodation that was much better than the cramped Type VIIs, in practice it was often at least as bad. Though their kill record was good, relatively few were built and they ceased to be built in January 1944.

The first batch, started in 1935, were the Type IXA (U37-44). The IXB followed (U64-65, 103-111, 122-124) with larger bunkers, and often with the 105 mm gun replaced by two pairs of 20 mm AA. The main production model was the IXC dating from 1940 (U65-68, 125-131, 153-166, 171-176, 501-524, 841-846, 853-858, 865-870, 877-881, 889-892, 1221-1238), with extended external tanks, much augmented AA armament and refitted with snort (Schnorkel). Two of these were transferred to Japan in 1943 and 1944. Different mainly in equipment, the IXC40 dated from the end of 1940 (U167–170, 183–194, 525–550, 801–806). Then followed the IXD long-range tanker (U180, 195), with 203 tons in its own bunkers and 252 tons of fuel for surface transfer to other submarines. Originally these had three pairs of high-speed diesels, but these proved unreliable and had to be replaced by one pair of slow-running engines of much lower power. To carry their load of oil they sacrificed their tubes and part of their battery capacity. They were supplanted by the important IXD2 class which was a fighting tanker powered by a 9-cylinder and a 6-cylinder diesel on each shaft, with double the power of what had become reclassified IXD1. The D2 class (U177–179, 181–182, 196–200, 847–852, 859–864, 871–876, 883–884, 886) had the remarkable bunker capacity of 442 tons, as well as six tubes and twenty-four torpedoes and with the option of carrying eight mine shafts, each with four mines, and only six torpedoes in the tubes (i.e., no reloads). Most were given numerous 20 mm AA in lieu of the 105 mm gun, and a snort (Schnorkel). Two were transferred to Japan in 1945. Popular name for the Type IX was Seekuh (sea cow) and the IXDs were Uberseekuh (overseas cow).

German Type XB

Not a success, these large mine-layers were clumsy and unpopular, and only eight were built (U116–119, 219–220, 233–234). Though all tubes were sacrificed other than two at the stern, sixty-two mines were carried in twenty-four external side shafts (two in each) and six forward internal shafts (three each). All were built in 1941, and were used chiefly as supply boats.

German Type XIV

A class of ten (U459–464, 487–490), these were called Milchkuh (milk cow) and were specially designed as long-range tanker and supply boats. Short and fat, they nevertheless behaved well and had large dead-weight capacity of 203 tons (own fuel) plus 432 tons (oil for transfer), as well as four externally stowed torpedoes. Their sole armament was one or two 37 mm guns and one to four 20 mm. With much heavier AA armament they might have lasted longer, but in fact all ten were sunk very quickly, mostly by air attack, because they were priority No 1 in the North Atlantic and they could not dive fast enough to escape. It was this problem of slow escape from the surface that killed the projected Type XV and Type XVI (5,000 tons) with three pressure hulls side-by-side.

German Type XVII (54)

As early as 1911 the Germans were conducting laboratory experiments with propulsion systems running on a closed cycle that did not breathe air, so that it would be possible to build a true submarine (one that was designed to stay submerged). By World War 2 the research had gathered momentum, and in 1940 trials began with the odd little V80.

This was powered by a single turbine running on the method developed by Prof. Hellmuth Walter. The latter was the father of the rocket engine used in the tailless Me163, easily the fastest warplane of World War 2. One of the propellants used in this rocket was T-stoff or concentrated hydrogen peroxide, which can readily decompose into free oxygen and superheated steam. For submarine propulsion, Walter proposed to use the peroxide alone, in a refined form called Perhydrol. Pumped from tanks and passed through a catalyst chamber it flashed into its constituents in a reaction chamber from which the hot products were expanded through a turbine. It was possible to sustain extremely high power from a compact and reliable plant, while consuming no air and leaving no trail in the sea. But fuel consumption was exceedingly high.

What spurred the Walter boat was the sudden terrible recognition in May 1943 of the fact that the VIIC was obsolete, and that the entire U-boat fleet would soon be destroyed by the aircraft and ships of the Allies. In 1940 the V80 had run submerged at an unprecedented 28 knots, but her range was a mere 58 miles. So as an operational U-boat the Type XVII was quickly planned, with a double pressure hull like a figure 8, the lower and smaller portion being occupied mainly by Perhydrol. Naturally these tall, narrow boats were not good at seakeeping, but their performance was impressive. Type XVIIA (U792-795), completed in

1943, reached 26 knots submerged with two turbines geared to one shaft, the 40 tons of Perhydrol giving a range at this speed of 80 miles. Next came Type XVIIB (U1405-1407) of 1944, with a single turbine and 55 tons of Perhydrol giving a range of 114 miles at 20 knots. There then followed a wealth of projects and part-finished prototypes, all of great technical interest and some truly impressive. One group, the XVIIK type, would have had a closed-cycle diesel fed by compressed air bottles and Ingolin fuel; another, the big XVIII, would have run 230 miles at up to 24 knots on three 5,000 h.p. Walter turbines. None reached the operational stage. In 1946 U1407, which had been scuttled at the German collapse, was salvaged and commissioned as HMS Meteorite. She helped in the design of the much improved Explorer (p.158).

German Type XXI (55)

Though the pace and success of Walter boats was remarkable, in view of the difficulties encountered, it was obvious that by 1944 few of these radical U-boats would be in service to meet Germany's urgent need. A possibly more logical answer to the problem of producing a new U-boat was to keep the figure-8 hull and use conventional diesel/electric propulsion, using the lower part of the hull mainly for extra batteries. Very quickly the Type XXI was designed in July-August 1943, and the result was a massive advance in submarine engineering. Though in no sense as radical as the Type XVII series, the XXI was not just better than the Type VIIC but of an order of technology and lethality that no submarine had ever before approached. To some degree this was just because the parts all fitted together on the drawing board beautifully, but had this design been done in 1940, as it could have been, the Allies might have lost the war.

Type XXI was far bigger than the VIIC. Only slightly longer, it was fatter and three times as deep, giving much more room inside. This room was put to good use, with three times as much battery capacity, giving a sustained submerged speed of 16 knots. When schnorkelling (snorting) at periscope depth it was possible to run at 12 knots instead of the previous 6 (imposed on the VIIC to prevent the snort (Schnorkel) being snapped off), and there were also silent creeping electric motors to steal away from a scene at 5 knots before starting the 16 knot dash. The large conning tower had become an enclosed, streamlined fin, with power-aimed AA cannon at each end fed by endless belts. Mechanical handling equipment speeded torpedo reloading, which in the old VIIC had been a long and exhausting struggle. The crew had air-conditioning and even a deep-freeze to keep food fresh. The hull was wholly welded from eight prefab. sections, and though big and complex the boat was planned for rapid production. Albert Speer's ministry was put in charge, and reported

twenty could be built each month. Blohm und Voss at Hamburg were given contracts for Type XXI boats numbered U2501–2761, with plans to build U2762–3000; AG Weser at Bremen were awarded U3001–3250, with plans to build U3251–3500; and Schichau at Danzig were awarded U3501–3750, with plans to build U3751–4000. Despite the fact that Germany was being pounded into rubble, with Hamburg in particular being a waste of charred ruins, construction of these large and very advanced vessels got under way at a remarkable rate, with almost all the work being done by foreign slave-labour, women and children, and very old or sick men —nearly all of them unskilled. The first XXI was launched at Hamburg on 17 July 1944, and soon Speer's target of twenty per month was being exceeded, with about 3 weeks being needed for basic manufacture, 2 weeks for assembly and another 2 weeks for fitting out. Ultimately about fifty-two boats were commissioned from Hamburg, forty-three from the Weser yard and thirty from Danzig, and many were attacked during trials; but only two left on patrol, at the final collapse. One, U2511, proved that this type of submarine would have been extremely formidable; but the commander had orders not to attack, and he returned to Bergen to surrender. The influence of these submarines can be seen in almost every subsequent design with conventional propulsion. The Soviet W (Whisky) class was almost a direct extrapolation.

German Type XXIII

Despite a wealth of projects and part-completed boats, the XXIII was the only other type of submarine actually to be completed for service in Nazi Germany. It was the Type XXI philosophy applied to a coastal submarine marking the barest minimum that could safely put to sea and perform a useful mission. Much smaller even than the baby Type IIs, it had a crew of 14 who literally rubbed elbows and had every excuse for displaying emotional tension. The two tubes were loaded from outside, there being no room for any reloads. Though capable of extremely rapid and cheap production, the XXIII was born into an environment of chaos and desperation and was unable to do more than score a few limited successes. Deutsche Werft at Hamburg delivered U2321-2331 and 2334-2372, while many were left unfinished at other yards of the same company; Germania delivered U2332-2333 and U4701-4712, and many hundreds were cancelled.

German midget submarines (56/57)

Rather surprisingly, the Germans almost ignored the concept of the human torpedo or one-man submarine until well into 1943. Then the possibility that such craft might have a role to play in the event of an Allied invasion of Europe, along the lines already carried out the previous year in North Africa, led to a reluctant authorisation of development of experimental prototypes. Quite

swiftly the work proliferated, and by the spring of 1944 there were more than a dozen small craft operating on trials, and it was widely believed by laymen that they would achieve great results. The Kriegsmarine were never enthusiastic, but sanctioned mass-production of the following types:

Biber (Beaver), a true one-man midget submarine, with fairly conventional hull and conning tower. It carried two torpedoes slung in recesses along the lower sides. About 324 were completed and 300 delivered by road or rail for use. Several made attacks after D-day (6 June 1944). On 29 December 1944 Biber-90 was discovered near the English coast with the operator apparently killed by carbon monoxide poisoning caused by the petrol engine. This surviving Biber is now in the Imperial War Museum, London.

Neger (Negro), a one-man device based on the body of a standard torpedo (G7e), carrying a second G7e underslung. Though a Plexiglas dome was fitted over the occupant he had no breathing equipment and could not dive for more than a few seconds. About 200 were completed, but no engineering records exist.

Marder (Marten) was very similar to Neger except that it did provide breathing equipment and could be dived in the normal way. About 300 were delivered, and a few were used operationally.

Mölch (Newt, Salamander) was a bigger device more akin to Biber, with a big cylindrical hull carrying electric batteries, and an operator at the back. Two G7e torpedoes were attached to external racks. About 390 were completed, mostly by Lubecker Flenderwerft.

Seehund (Seal), distinguished by receiving the U-boat type number of XXVIIB, was easily the biggest and best of the K-craft, and had a crew of two. It had a proper hull, diesel/electric propulsion and a screw discharging through a Kort nozzle with rudders and 'elevator' planes. Two torpedoes were carried on external pylons, and the commander even had a periscope. About 250, numbered from U5001, were completed, mostly at Germania, Howaldtswerke, Schichau and Klockner, while contracts up to U6351 were scrapped incomplete or cancelled.

British S class (58/59)
This very important and successful class was a bold attempt to carry out the overseas patrol function with a submarine much smaller than the trusty L class. Though actually 1 ft fatter in beam, the S class were much shorter and also were updated in technology and convenience. More were built than any other Royal Navy class. The first group were designed in the late 1920s and commissioned in the five years from 1932: Sturgeon, Swordfish, Seahorse, Starfish, Sealion, Shark, Sunfish, Snapper, Seawolf, Spearfish, Sterlet.

In the big rearmament programmes of 1936 onwards the smaller U class was introduced for coastal patrol and training, and additional S ships were ordered. This was because the S had proved most suitable for operations in the North Sea. The first five of the new batch—Safari, Sahib, Saracen, Satyr and Sceptre—resembled the previous ones, and were completed in 1938. The remainder were 9 ft longer, had a different conning tower and, except for the final batch at the end of the war, a seventh tube added pointing aft. Names were: Sea Dog, Sibyl, Sea Rover, Sea Nymph, Seraph, Shakespeare, P222, Sickle, Simoon, Sirdar, Spiteful, Splendid, Sportsman, Stoic, Stonehenge, Storm, Stratagem, Strongbow, Spark, Scythian, Stubborn, Surf, Syrtis, Shalimar, Scotsman, Sea Devil, Spirit, Statesman, Sturdy, Stygian, Subtle, Supreme, Sea Scout, Selene, Seneschal, Sentinel, Saga, Scorcher, Sidon, Sleuth, Solent, Spearhead, Springer, Spur, Sanguine.

British U and V classes (60/61/62)
The extremely successful U class was designed in 1934 as replacement for the fast-vanishing H class as the standard coastal patrol and training submarine of the Royal Navy, and the contrast was immense. Longer but having the same hull diameter, the U class were immeasurably superior in interior arrangement and equipment, and introduced an improved deck gun. The first six, commissioned in 1938–39, were Umpire, Una, Union, Undaunted, Urchin and Urge. Subsequently two of the bow tubes were deleted, leaving a total

of four, and the length was cut by 6 ft. The modified ships were: Undine, Unity, Ursula, Unbeaten, Unique, Upholder, Upright, Usk and Utmost.

For cost/effectiveness it is doubtful that any submarines in history can equal these hard-worked ships, which operated far from their friendly coast in Norway and throughout the Mediterranean. The Malta Flotilla, especially, performed countless great feats of courage and endurance; Upholder (Lt-Cdr Wanklyn VC) probably has the finest fighting record of any Allied submarine of World War 2, one of her early kills, on 25 May 1941, being the troopship *Conte Rosse* with over 1,200 members of the Afrika Corps on board.

From late 1940 deliveries proceeded on a second group with a hull of the original 196 ft length (but still only four tubes) and a cleaner flared bow: Uproar, P32, P33, Ultimatum, Umbra, P36, Unbending, P38, P39, Uredd, Unbroken, Unison, United, Unrivalled, Unruffled, Dolfijn (RNethN), P48, Unseen, Dzik (Polish N), Ultor, Unshaken, Unsparing, Usurper, Universal, Untamed (lost in 1943 but later recovered and recommissioned as Vitality), Untiring, Varangian, Uther, Unswerving, Vandal, Upstart and Varne (RNethN, later renamed Ula). United, Unison and Unbroken were in 1944 transferred to the Soviet Union as V-2, V-3 and V-4.

In 1943 the V class was introduced, with a more powerful diesel

to improve surface speed despite a further 10 ft increase in length: Upshot, Urtica, Vagabond, Vampire, Variance, Varne (after renaming of the original ship of that name), Veldt (recommissioned into RHellenicN as Pipinos), Vengeful, Venturer, Vigorous, Viking, Vineyard, Virtue, Virulent, Visigoth, Vivid, Volatile, Voracious, Vortex, Votary, Vox and Vulpine.

British T class (63)

The overseas patrol category had numerically fallen off considerably between the wars, and during the 1930s construction had concentrated upon the small S class. The T class was planned in the mid-1930s as the standard future large submarine for 42-day patrols. Despite the much higher unit price compared with the S class, the growing threat of war at last opened the purse-strings and made it possible to plan a major force. No fewer than twenty-two of these fine submarines were ordered in 1935–37, and these were commissioned in 1937–39 under the following names: Triton, Thetis, Tribune, Trident, Triumph, Taku, Tarpon, Thistle, Tigris, Triad, Truant, Tuna, Talisman, Tetrarch, Torbay, Tempest, Thorn, Thrasher, Traveller, Trooper, Trusty and Turbulent.

One of this group, Thetis, sailed from Cammell Laird's yard at Birkenhead on the morning of 1 June 1939 for her check dive and trim test prior to handover. She had on board her crew of fifty-three plus fifty passengers (officers, observers, RN engineers and yard technicians and management). She was very reluctant to submerge. The six bow tubes were checked; four were correctly found empty and then the Nos 5 and 6 were tested to confirm that these two each contained 800 lb of sea-water. The test cock from No 6 squirted water. No 5, however, emitted no water, and so was apparently empty. The only way to check was to open it. After much wrenching, the door was opened—and the sea roared in. The bow cap had been left open, and the vital test cock was blocked with paint. A stupid type of watertight door could not be closed because it was jammed by one of its clips, and with two compartments flooded Thetis dived nose-first to the seabed 160 ft below. Even though her stern was clear of the surface she was not found for a whole day, and, though four men managed to escape, the terrible official bungling caused the remainder of the men on board to die within 48 hours.

In November the stricken ship was raised, and after a refit she was commissioned in November 1940 as Thunderbolt—with a diagonal rusty line on her hull that could not be hidden. After good service she was finally sunk by the Italians in March 1943.

Though almost as long as the S class, the T ships were slimmer and had appreciably less displacement. They were the last RN submarines designed for overseas patrol to have range insufficient for the Pacific, and in later years their speed was also to be judged inadequate. On the other hand they were heavily armed with ten tubes, and an eleventh was added in the second, larger, group of these vessels constructed after World War 2 had begun and delivered in 1942–44: P311, Tactician, Taurus, Templar, Thule, Tireless, Token, Trespasser, Truculent, Tudor, Talent, Tally-Ho, Tantalus, Tantivy, Telemachus, Terrapin, Thorough, Tiptoe, Totem, Tradewind, Trenchant, Trump, Truncheon, Tabard, Taciturn, Tapir, Tarn, Tasman, Teredo, Thermopylae and Turpin. Most of these had welded hulls.

Numbering fifty-three in all, this was the largest class of big ocean-going submarines ever built for the Royal Navy, and their exploits in World War 2 are an important part of that Service's history. From the technical viewpoint they are also of uncommon interest. As originally built, the first batch, which had riveted hulls, had six bow tubes and two more above the pressure hull, one each side of the conning tower. They were arranged to fire ahead, angled out at $7\frac{1}{2}$ deg. and firing torpedoes set to turn through $7\frac{1}{2}$ deg. to run dead ahead but 350 yds (1,050 ft) apart. Later these tubes were removed, and either two or three were added in the external deck casing aft, firing astern. In the bows the original six tubes were supplemented by two more fitted externally above the pressure hull in an added casing, angled slightly downwards. These were then removed from many boats, but during the war a large bulbous bow tank was added with two extra tubes, restoring the total number to ten or eleven. Thus, many T class had five external tubes, which could not be reloaded at sea.

After 1945 plans were laid for modification of the survivors. Not very much could be done with the riveted-hull boats, but five—Tapir, Tireless, Talent, Teredo, Token— were streamlined and completely refitted with six bow tubes only (no guns or external tubes), modern sonar and a fin-type conning tower. In 1951–56 eight of the welded-hull boats were completely rebuilt. Their hulls were cut in two and new sections were spliced in adding 12, 14 or 20 ft to the length. Battery capacity was enormously increased, and doubled diesel-electric drives were fitted giving twice the previous submerged speed. At the same time, noise was dramatically reduced by stream-lining, and sensing and detection equipment was updated. The eight thus converted were Tabard, Trump, Truncheon, Tiptoe, Taci-turn, Thermopylae, Totem and Turpin.

British X, XE, XT Midget classes
Though often mooted, no navy had commissioned a true midget sub-marine by the outbreak of World War 2; but at that time the Italians were well advanced in preparation and so was the Royal Navy. Following careful consideration of the idea, the first midget was laid down in 1939. Instead of launching torpedoes it was to be a means of conveyance for highly trained divers who, when close under the hull of the target vessel riding at anchor or tied up at its base, would place demolition charges along the enemy bottom before re-entering the sub-marine to return. At best the scheme was hazardous, and to attack a major fighting ship in a well protected and alert base posed formidable problems. Such an at-tack would have to be made after possibly spending more than a week in an interior measuring 35 ft by 5 ft wide by 5 ft high, in a submarine that rode a rough sea very badly. In any case, range was very limited, and operations were to be supported by full-size submarines for towing and crew rescue.

After delays the first midget was on trial off Scotland in October 1942, being commissioned as X3 (X1 see p.113; X2 was a captured Italian submarine). A further seven were built, the obvious initial target being Tirpitz, holed up in Alten Fjord. In Operation Source, X5 to X10 inclusive were towed for eight days across the North Sea, boarded by their operational crews and, despite terrible difficulties, caused heavy damage on 22 September 1943 which prevented Tir-pitz from ever sailing (she was finally sunk by the RAF). XT1 to XT6 were used for training, X20 to X25 were a second batch, and the final operational version was the flush-decked XE1 to XE9 and XE11 and 12, designed for the Far East. They had air-conditioning and much extra stowage space, as well as an air lock so that one of the crew could place limpet charges on the enemy hull. On 31 July 1945

XE3 was squeezed in under the bottom of the Japanese heavy cruiser Takao in Johore Strait and escaped before the charges went off, sinking the 11,000 ton vessel.

In 1954–5 four improved craft were built, X51 Stickleback (later Swedish Spiggen), X52 Shrimp, X53 Sprat (later US Navy) and X54 Minnow. They incorporated numerous detail improvements.

British Chariot torpedoes (49)

Curiously, the Royal Navy never attempted to develop any midget device that actually launched a torpedo. The Chariots, copied from the Italian Maiali, were electric vehicles manned by a crew of two, who sat externally, and attempted to fasten their bow charge on to the enemy hull. In Norway the water was found to be so cold that the crew became incapacitated, but in the Mediterranean results were impressive. The most notable successes of the British Chariots were the sinkings of three Italian cruisers: Ulpio Traiano at Palermo on 3 January 1943, Bolzano at La Spezia on 21 June 1944 and Gorizia at La Spezia on 26 June 1944.

British A class

Sudden emergence of the Pacific Ocean as a major battleground in December 1941 demanded urgent rethinking of Royal Navy submarine policy. None of the existing British submarines had really adequate range, and within weeks the decision was taken to design a completely new class of submarine

having much greater range and also increased surface speed. The opportunity was also taken to introduce major technical advances, of which the most important was an all-welded hull. Another was the 'Snort' (Schnorkel), which the Royal Navy—more or less enjoying command of the sea surface—had previously considered not worth having. The result was one of the best of all 'traditional' types of pre-nuclear submarine, with a high flared bow for excellent sea performance, formidable armament of ten 21 in. tubes and appreciably reduced underwater noise level.

Skipping the letters X, Y and Z, the new class had names beginning with A: Acheron, Aeneas, Affray, Alaric, Alcide, Alderney, Alliance, Ambush, Anchorite, Amphion, Andrew, Artemis, Artful, Astute, Auriga and Aurochs. More than twenty other submarines of this class were under contract when World War 2 ended and they were cancelled. The A vessels made only a minor contribution right at the end of World War 2, being delivered between 1945 and 1948.

In the immediate post-war years these were the leading type of RN submarine, and several variants were exported. One of this class, Affray, left Portsmouth on 16 April 1951 on a training cruise, diving at 9 p.m. that evening in the extreme western part of the English Channel. She vanished, and a search was rendered very difficult by the fact the commander's brief was a very wide-ranging one. With a full crew aboard plus twenty-three submarine officers under training and some RM Commandos—seventy-five men in all—it was imperative to effect rescue quickly. In the event she was not found until late in June, by an underwater TV camera searching north of Guernsey in 278 ft of water. Her snort was snapped off, but no explanation was ever given as to why she sank, why nobody escaped or why she was never salvaged. She was the last RN submarine to be lost.

From 1967 these fine submarines have been scrapped, sold or rebuilt with a more streamlined hull carrying a conning-tower sail 26·5 ft high. In 1972 Aeneas was hired by Vickers for successful trials of the SLAM (Submarine-Launched Anti-aircraft Missile), a four-barrel cluster of Blowpipe guided missiles having high lethality against low-flying aircraft, and which in the course of time is likely to be widely adopted for submarine defence. By 1975 all this class had been stricken except for Andrew, the submarine which in 1953 set the Royal Navy's snorting record by a submerged 15-day passage from Bermuda to England.

THE MODERN ERA

Since World War 2 man's world has been prevented from having a major all-out war because of the annihilating threat of nuclear weapons. These were originally delivered by aircraft, but during the 1950s renewed efforts were made in the United States and the Soviet Union to develop nuclear-armed missiles that could be launched from submarines. At first such missiles were of the 'cruise' type, resembling miniature aircraft and flying an essentially flat trajectory through the atmosphere, propelled by an engine and supported by a wing. In the Soviet Union cruise missiles remain important to this day in naval operations, but the United States —certainly unwisely—dropped them in 1957 and concentrated entirely upon the ballistic missile. This has no wings, is launched more or less vertically, and accelerates up through the atmosphere so that, when the final stage of rocket propulsion is cut off, the warhead(s) continue in an arching ballistic trajectory for hundreds or thousands of miles to the target.

This development was the most significant in the history of the submarine. 'Mating the shark with the eagle' as an American admiral called it, took the submarine entirely out of its previous narrow role of ship-killer and made it the prime instrument of deterrence. Today submarines far larger than any other kind of warship, save only aircraft carriers, can voyage silently to any place on Earth and there threaten the whole territory of potential enemies. They can, upon secure command, launch up to sixteen (soon, twenty-four) missiles from deep beneath the ocean surface. Each missile can carry several warheads, each independently targeted. Each warhead can destroy a city.

Development of the original class of Polaris-firing US Navy submarines was amazingly rapid, spurred by the dynamic energy of Admiral H. G. Rickover who had earlier masterminded the development of submarine nuclear propulsion. Construction of a fleet of forty-one giant Fleet Ballistic Missile Submarines appeared to give the US Navy an unassailable lead; but, despite an initial inferiority in missile technology, the Soviet Union closed the gap and then, in 1971, drew ahead of the US nuclear submarine force. Rickover commented in that year 'Numerical superiority . . . does not tell the whole story. Weapon systems, speed, depth, detection devices, quietness of operation, and crew performance all make a significant contribution to the effectiveness of a submarine force. From what we have been able to learn during the past year, the Soviets have attained equality in a number of these characteristics, and superiority in some.'

This fact alone is staggering, and must sharply interest everyone in the West. At the same time, one probably ought not to regard the Russians as a race of supermen. They have accomplished much in a short time, but it has been done only at the expense of severely limited expenditure on non-military matters. The Soviet Union's defence funding has been a great burden, and the vast sums involved have perhaps not always been spent wisely. There has been a very pronounced tendency towards sudden crash programmes which have caused a great deal of effort to be devoted to hardware which within a year or two looked notably unattractive. Good examples are the Whisky single-cylinder, Whisky twin-cylinder and Golf I and II submarine classes, which were hasty botches suffering from severe operational drawbacks. At the same time, one wistfully wishes the same kind of military money was available in the West, where years are spent on paper studies and evaluations while inflation puts each proposed weapon system further and further out of reach.

Submarines, though far more lethal than before, are also far more costly. Except for nuclear super-carriers they are man's most expensive weapons. This is largely because of the development some twenty-five years ago of submarine nuclear propulsion. This was one of the greatest of all revolutions in submarine technology, and though it demands large and expensive designs it offers benefits beyond price. At last the submariner has all the underwater energy supplies he needs, for as long as he wishes, without any requirement for any connection with the atmosphere. As a result today's nuclear submarines are true underwater craft, needing never to surface except on return to port or for a deliberate operational reason. They have very high underwater speed, making them hard to catch; and in the West, at least, this speed has been achieved with increasing silence of operation. Coupled with air-conditioning and a fantastic improvement in living conditions today's submarines are the greatest possible contrast with their predecessors.

US Guppy conversions (41/68)

At the end of World War 2 the US Navy naturally had a huge surplus of submarines, with over 100 more in various stages of completion at yards all over the nation. Nearly all the uncompleted boats were cancelled, and for more than two years no money was voted for purchase of any new submarines. Large numbers of boats were mothballed, and a smaller quantity were disposed of by sale to friendly nations, gifts to allies, by consumption as targets and by conversion for various research, trials or training roles. Meanwhile great attention was paid to improving the technology of the submarine. For the long term the brightest prospect appeared to be nuclear power, but the pioneer work of the Germans (Type XXI in particular) was immediately relevant. In 1947 extensive engineering studies culminated in the start of a major conversion programme for improving the fighting performance, especially when submerged, of existing US Navy submarines. The project was named Guppy, from the initials Greater Underwater Propulsion Program.

The Guppy programme was undertaken over a period of fifteen years, in several stages. All conversions were originally vessels of the Balao and Tench classes, with a few Gato submarines in the first (Guppy I) programme in 1947-49. Details of individual boats are too numerous to list, but the basic philosophy was one of increasing underwater power and reducing drag. Surface propulsion was left at three or four of the standard 1,600 h.p. diesels, driving the original twin shafts, but all boats were fitted with a snorkel. Electric storage capacity was considerably increased by the introduction of an improved 126-cell battery installation. Completely new electric motors were fitted for underwater propulsion, one on each shaft, each with a rating of 2,700 h.p. (roughly double that of the original motors). The hull was completely stripped, overhauled and rebuilt with a smooth exterior, bulged bow and much new equipment, usually including one, two or three projecting PUFF (Passive Underwater Fire-control Feasibility system) aerials, usually of the BQG-4 type, a system of fixing target position by passive acoustic triangulation. The BQR-2 array sonar was also usually installed, as well as various types of radar and countermeasures. All deck guns were removed. In most Guppy conversions the conning tower was removed and replaced by a streamlined sail of lightweight alloys and plastics.

Several submarines progressed through two or even three consecutive Guppy conversions. The total number of conversions approached 100, and they kept an active force of some fifty vessels in active service over a period of some twenty years. By 1975 almost all had been stricken or passed on to friendly nations, and the last World War 2 submarine of all, *Tigrone*, was decommissioned on 27 June 1975.

USS Albacore (40)

Though never intended as an operational combat submarine, this vessel has proved as significant to submarine technology as any in history. She resulted from the extensive hydrodynamic test programme undertaken at the time of the Guppy laboratory investigations immediately following World War 2. Though such research could have been done at any time, it was not until the late 1940s that the optimum shape for a submarine, and the best arrangement for its control surfaces for both surface and underwater running, was finally discovered. The result was found to be a hull much fatter than normal, with a relatively bluff bow, circular section, long tapering rear section and the smoothest possible exterior. The traditional conning tower was replaced by a slim structure called a sail (or fin), roughly resembling the dorsal fin of a fish.

This new shape was tested full-scale by this submarine, laid down at Portsmouth (New Hampshire) Navy Yard in March 1952 and commissioned on 5 December 1953. Though having the same maximum beam as the big wartime classes (just over 27 ft) she was 100 ft shorter, and though she had enormous installed power there was no shortage of pundits who predicted she would be slower than the Guppy conversions. In fact her performance was a revelation, an unfolding of totally new horizons in the technology of the submerged submarine. For the first time one saw a submarine that was not merely a surface vessel able to submerge but a vehicle obviously intended to travel under water rather than along the surface. There was no familiar deck; instead Albacore had a sloping back like a whale. There were no significant projections; even cleats were recessed. Unlike most contemporary US submarines she had only a single propeller.

On her early trials she established an underwater speed record of 33 knots (over 38 m.p.h.). Gradually her helmsman learned to do things never before attempted: eventually she was recognised to be a true underwater vehicle, able to travel in any direction, to make tight banked turns and even to loop. Obviously, from now onwards submarines were going to be 'flown' in three dimensions, like an aircraft, and the helmsman was accordingly seated at aircraft-type controls and strapped in.

During her active life (1953–72) Albacore was constantly testing new configurations and equipment. A great deal of effort was at first devoted to the back end, with different arrangements of fin, horizontal planes and propeller. Eventually the best scheme was found to be with the propeller overhung behind the control surfaces with the shaft emerging from the tip of the hull. Later still the vertical and horizontal planes were replaced by a symmetrical 'tail' of X shape. The only major configuration not explored was main diving planes on the sail, though she tried various dorsal or sail-mounted rudders. At one time Albacore had a ring of hydraulically opened 'dive brakes'.

USS Tang and developments (40/41, 64/65, 66/67)

USS Tang gave her name to the first class of new post-war submarines to be built in the United States. They were conventional clean vessels, utilising all the German technology simultaneously being used in the Guppy programme, and in addition having a radical new diesel for surface propulsion with four banks of four 2-stroke cylinders and unprecedented ratio of power to weight. Eventually this engine failed to achieve satisfactory reliability, and in the late 1950s the four in which it was fitted—Tang, Trigger, Trout and Wahoo—were re-engined with a standard lightweight diesel as fitted to the remaining two, Gudgeon and Harder. They were also lengthened and modernised, and were subsequently lengthened again, adding 19 ft to their original 269 ft. With six tubes for'ard and two aft, they were efficient attack vessels but all were stricken by the end of 1975.

Darter was a later submarine developed with specially quiet machinery, but overtaken by new technology in hull shape and propulsion. She was timed four years after the Tangs, being laid down in

1954 and commissioned in 1956. At the same time some very similar submarines were laid down which were completed as missile submarines. Two further vessels, Sailfish and Salmon, were completed to a considerably larger design in 1956 as radar pickets with large surveillance radars and interiors fitted as air control centres for use in remote battle areas. These two submarines remain in service after conversion to function as ordinary attack submarines, and are believed to have been the biggest non-nuclear submarines of the post-war period.

The Darter submarines that emerged as missile-launchers were Grayback, laid down in July 1954 and Growler which followed seven months later. Basically they had the same hull of 27 ft $2\frac{1}{2}$ in. beam, with flat Fairbanks Morse diesels and two electric motors as the Darter and the Tang class, but in 1955 both were selected as carriers for the first naval cruise missiles to be planned for operational service. During the first half of the 1950s guided missiles were being avidly developed for many purposes. The US Air Force introduced the Matador as a sophisticated successor to the German 'V-1' in the form of a jet-propelled miniature aircraft carrying a large conventional or nuclear warhead and able to navigate to a distant target. Running a little later in timing, the US Navy developed the Regulus. To carry Regulus, Grayback and Growler were lengthened by 50 ft, fitted with twin missile containers on the bows, with a launch rail leading aft for rocket-boosted take-off, and equipped with very comprehensive navigation systems so that the launch position could always be determined within an error-limit of half a mile.

These two submarines entered service in 1959, each able to carry and launch four Regulus I missiles. Two smaller and older submarines, Tunny and Barbero, were each converted to carry and fire two missiles, while in 1956 the Navy was authorised to build a much larger nuclear-powered submarine to carry two of the longer and much more formidable Regulus II missiles. This nuclear vessel, the 5,000 ton Halibut, was held up by cancellation of the Regulus II—not because of failure of the missile but because of the obviously greater 'penetrability' of ballistic missiles— and she eventually commissioned in January 1960 carrying five Regulus Is. All five missile submarines, classed as SSGs (Halibut: SSGN), served until the Regulus missile was judged obsolete in 1964. Barbero and Tunny were stricken (Tunny serving for a while as a transport), Halibut was used for deep-submergence operations and Growler was placed in reserve. Grayback was converted in 1967 into an amphibious transport submarine, the conversion costing much more than the original price as a missile carrier. Lengthened by 12 ft, Grayback carries sixty-seven Marines or other amphibious warfare troops and their landing craft or Swimmer Delivery Vehicles.

She retains her torpedo tubes and navigation systems.

USS Barracuda (65)

For forty years the US Navy has acquired virtually no small submarines. The exception is this small post-war boat, laid down by Electric Boat in 1949. She was intended as a small, quiet and nimble anti-submarine platform, lightly armed with two tubes at each end and with much less range and endurance than other US submarines. She was give inadequate propulsive power, her submerged speed being a mere eight knots, and after wasting most of her first ten years she was re-graded SST-3, a training submarine, in 1959. In 1972 she was again regraded, to SS-T3, giving the appearance of being in the attack force. This was just so that the number of US attack submarines could on paper be increased by one. She appears to have no operational mission and may be stricken by the time this book is published.

USS Nautilus (69)

In 1930 Nautilus was the world's biggest submarine (p.119). Her namesake of the 1950s was an even more important and historic vessel, for she was not only again the biggest but also the first nuclear submarine—in fact, the first nuclear powered vehicle of any kind. In theory nuclear energy was the ideal form of submarine propulsion, for it offered almost limitless energy on each loading of fuel, for sustained high speed and for auxiliary purposes such as air-conditioning,

without needing any supply of fresh air. Thus, a submarine using such propulsion need never surface, save to change over tired crews. This promised a complete revolution in submarine capability.

In August 1949 the US Chief of Naval Operations issued a formal requirement for a nuclear submarine, with an in-service date of January 1955. It was an ambitious goal, for no nuclear reactor capable of propelling a submarine existed. As in so many great enterprises it was the relentless drive of one man that forced the programme to move fast: Capt. (later Admiral) Hyman G. Rickover, head of the newly formed Naval Reactors Branch of the US Atomic Energy Commission. By 1950 the decision had been taken to build two submarines. One would be powered by a pressurised water reactor (PWR), in which the hot core of fissile enriched uranium fuel would be cooled by a closed circuit of water under very high pressure, which would expand into superheated steam as it passed through the propulsion turbines. It would then be condensed back to water, rejecting heat to the sea, and used again. No material would be discharged by the submarine other than warm sea-water. The rival reactor would be cooled by a closed circuit filled with liquid sodium metal, which could extract heat at a much higher rate and at a higher temperature but appeared to pose formidable development difficulties.

In the event the liquid-sodium reactor, known as the Submarine

Intermediate Reactor (SIR) did take longer to develop. Engineered mainly at the Knolls Atomic Power Laboratory, and tested as a complete submarine propulsion system at West Milton, New York, the SIR finally propelled the submarine Seawolf on 21 January 1957. After two years of generally problem-ridden steaming, Seawolf docked and refitted with PWR propulsion.

From the start the PWR Submarine Thermal Reactor (STR) looked the best bet, even though theoretically less efficient than the difficult liquid sodium. Contractor for the PWR submarine, SSN 571 Nautilus, was Electric Boat; contractor for the PWR was Westinghouse. The latter built a complete submarine propulsion system at the Atomic Energy Commission facility at Arco, Idaho. On 14 June 1952 President Harry S. Truman signed his name on the submarine's keel plate. On 21 January 1954 Nautilus was launched. Spurred on by Rickover and by the brilliant Electric Boat general manager, Carleton Shugg, hired from the Atomic Energy Commission, she was commissioned on 30 September 1954. On 17 January 1955 her first commander sent the famous signal 'Underway on nuclear power'. She also had an emergency diesel, but never used it in earnest. On her first loading of fuel Nautilus, by far the largest submarine built up to that time, steamed 62,560 miles. On the second load she went 93,000 miles. The third fuelling sent her well over 150,000 miles.

Included in the first fuelling's mileage was an historic 1958 trip from Pearl Harbor, Hawaii, under the Arctic ice, and directly under the geographic North Pole, to Portland, England. This was a hint of what submarines would be capable of in future.

US Barbel class

Though only three of these attack submarines were built they are significant in that, as the last non-nuclear submarines constructed for the US Navy, they give an indication of the definitive potential of the conventionally propelled submarine with the technology of the 1950s. Their hulls incorporated all the results of the early years of research with Albacore, and had the teardrop form (though with a flat deck) with single propeller on the centre-line. They even went beyond Albacore in having the main diving planes moved from the front hull, where they were at first, to a position 12 ft up the front of the streamlined sail fin. Model research had revealed that, at least for an attack submarine, this position was preferable and conferred the best attainable manoeuvrability in the vertical plane, and the improved behaviour of the modified Barbels caused this to become the standard arrangement in later American submarines. An even more important innovation was the arrangement of the interior to have an attack centre, where were grouped all the sensor outputs, displays, systems and position information, and controls for the vessel and weapons.

This co-ordinated centre was found to be a great advantage and to impose no penalty on use of space, and it was another feature of all subsequent US submarines.

US Skate class

Authorised in 1955 and 1956, before Nautilus had gone to sea, these four attack submarines were the first nuclear-powered production craft in history. They were also by far the smallest. One of the supposed disadvantages of nuclear propulsion is that it demands a very large vessel to accommodate the large and heavy shielded reactor and associated heat-exchange systems, and in the Skates attempts were made to develop a nuclear-propulsion system of minimum size. Rather remarkably, the resulting submarine was no larger than the Tang and similar classes. Their hulls were of the traditional Guppy kind, with twin screws, bow diving planes and pre-Albacore profile. Skate and Sargo differed from Swordfish and Seadragon in the engineering design and arrangement of their Westinghouse propulsion plant, though both schemes worked well. With these ships most of the possibilities of remote and prolonged-submergence operation were explored in 1958–60, ready for use in the much larger and faster attack submarines that followed.

USS Triton

Laid down on 29 May 1956, this monster is believed to have been the longest submarine in history (she is probably just overtaken by the Soviet Deltas) and at the time of her building was also by far the largest. Her purpose was to serve as a radar picket to protect surface task forces by cruising 100 or more miles ahead and keeping ceaseless watch for hostile aircraft. When she was built the power required for her propulsion demanded two reactors, which partly explains her size. The rather unusual power plant, with twin S4G pressurised-water reactors, was designed by Knolls Atomic Power Laboratory and built by General Electric. In service, from November 1959, she proved much less troublesome than one might have expected, and she soon made many fine submerged voyages of which the greatest was a complete trip round the world under water in 1960, a 41,500-mile journey taking 83 days at about 18 knots. In 1961 aerial surveillance could be done better by Airborne Early Warning (AEW) aircraft, and Triton's big radar was removed. She then served as an attack submarine, and when the cost of converting her into a secure undersea national command post was found to exceed her original cost of $109 million she was mothballed in 1969.

USS Halibut

In the early 1950s the US Navy planned a major force of cruise-type missiles, starting with Regulus I. This was to be followed by the supersonic Regulus II, and Halibut was authorised in 1956 as the first of a class of very large diesel-electric submarines to carry and fire two

Regulus IIs each. She was planned essentially as a secure launch platform, without much emphasis on underwater performance, and as a result had a large hull of traditional type filled with extensive navigation equipment and carrying a very large missile hangar ahead of the fin. In 1956 her design was altered to have nuclear propulsion, and she was finally completed in late 1959 with one of the S3W reactors of the kind fitted to Skate and Sargo. By this time Regulus II had been cancelled; she commissioned on 4 January 1960 and was rearranged to carry five Regulus Is. Although probably the slowest nuclear submarine ever built, Halibut (SSGN 587) was quite successful, and though noisy underwater could pack a formidable punch over a radius of 500 miles. In 1965 the US Navy de-activated the Regulus system, and after reclassification as an attack submarine Halibut found useful employment as mother vehicle to the Deep Submergence Rescue Vehicle (DSRV) and other submersibles, which she can carry on her afterdeck and retrieve after use.

US Skipjack class (70)

With this class of attack submarine the US Navy at last brought together the two giant forward strides in submarine technology, the spindle hull and nuclear propulsion. As a result they were the fastest submarines ever placed in combat service by the US Navy (until the recent Los Angeles class) and not least of their innovations

was the introduction of an excellent 'second-generation' reactor system, the Westinghouse-built S5W, driving a single propeller at the tip of the hull. So efficient was this propulsion system that it was used for every subsequent US Navy submarine for the next twenty years, except for Narwhal. Skipjack set the pattern in many other ways, with sail-mounted planes, all tubes at the bow, a standardised AS sensing display and control centre, and several features still classified.

With this class the US Navy enlarged the industrial base for submarine construction, with five shipyards for the six boats. All six were delayed by the crash programme to build SSBN Polaris submarines. The third of the class, Scorpion, was in fact renumbered from SSN 589 to SSBN 598 while under construction, was cut in two and grossly extended to become George Washington, the first SSBN. Scorpion was then laid down a second time, with the original number 589; and superstitious sailors will ponder on the fact she was lost with all hands while on a routine crossing of the Atlantic. The others of this class are Shark, Scamp, Sculpin and Snook.

USS Tullibee

Originally planned as a 1,000-ton attack submarine, this interesting vessel remained a 'one-off' research platform for an anti-submarine submarine, and though doubled in size to take nuclear propulsion is still the smallest nuclear vessel of all. Her hull is a kind of thin-spindle form, much more slender than that of all other post-1956 US Navy submarines, and she is driven by an extremely compact, low-power PWR system by Combustion Engineering. By far the most significant contribution made by Tullibee was the proving of an entirely rearranged sensing and armament system for AS use. Ideally the entire bow hemisphere needs to be devoted to sonar and other sensing systems, and in Tullibee this was done for the first time. The tubes thus had to go elsewhere, and the answer chosen with this vessel was left and right pairs of tubes angled diagonally outwards amidships. Another important innovation was that her nuclear-heated steam turbine drives a generator for electric final drive. This seems an unnecessarily complicated scheme, but elimination of the main reduction gear dramatically quietened Tullibee and showed the way to further improvements. She has an Autonetics Ships Inertial Navigation System (SINS), but is limited in performance and cannot catch hostile submarines.

US Permit class

During construction of the Skipjack class it became evident that a better attack submarine could be created, and this very important class, originally named for the lead-ship Thresher, is the result. Considerably bigger than the Skipjacks, they are at least as fast on identical propulsion and have the new arrangement of bow sonar arrays and amidships tubes, firing the new Subroc ASW missile. In addition to the BQQ-2 system they also have the advanced BQX-5 (formerly BQS-13DNA) active/passive sonar for long-range detection. Ships of this class differ appreciably. Many names were changed during construction, among them Plunger, Barb and Pollack which, with Dace, were originally authorised as Regulus II missile carriers. So that the diving planes could be more effective at periscope depth the sails of Flasher, Gato and Greenling were extended upwards to 21 ft, while Jack has a novel propulsion system with contra-rotating steam turbines directly driving small-diameter co-axial propellers.

Loss of Thresher, the lead ship, was the most dramatic submarine disaster of modern times. On trials after her first major overhaul, on 10 April 1963, she was engaged in deep diving trials 200 miles out from New England when she dived steeply out of control. Before she could be righted she plunged to a depth where her hull collapsed. It was this tragedy which spurred the dramatic increase in funding to explore the deep oceans and, at the same time, reduce the likelihood of losing further submarine crews.

US Sturgeon class

Natural successors to the Permits, the thirty-seven members of this very large and important class of attack submarine differ only in detail design and equipment. They incorporate the tall sail introduced with the three 'Advanced Permit' submarines, and also have BQS-8 under-ice sonar and provision for driving the diving planes to the vertical for breaking up through a thick ice layer. In service these have proved very successful submarines, though their construction was long and costly and resulted in startling differences in industrial perform-ance becoming painfully evident, with some contractors taking less than two years from keel-laying to commissioning and others taking more than seven. New weapon equipment includes the BPS-114 surveillance radar and, as a minor modification, provision to carry the Harpoon missile.

US Fleet Ballistic Missile Submarines (71/72/73)

No weapon system in history has been introduced more boldly, nor had so dramatic an effect on the entire strategy of warfare, as the US Fleet Ballistic Missile System (FBMS). Nor, having regard to its enormous extent and completely new technology, has one been designed, developed and deployed with such astonishing rapidity. It was natural that submarines should be developed to fire guided missiles; such proposals were made in Nazi Germany and came to fruition with cruise missiles in the early 1950s. Where the FBMS differed was that this was a global deterrent system able to menace the entire country of any hostile nation, except (at first) for central Asia, and the missiles could be launched from a secure and unknown position deep within the ocean depth.

At first, in 1955, the US Navy was teamed with the Army in the development of an IRBM (Inter-mediate-Range Ballistic Missile) called Jupiter. Propelled by liquid oxygen and RP-1 kerosene, this was a 60 ft weapon capable of projecting an early thermonuclear warhead a distance of 1,500 nautical miles (1,727 miles). Deployment aboard surface vessels was difficult enough, but submarine-based Jupiters posed severe problems. A design was prepared for a 10,000-ton sub-marine, powered by two Nautilus reactors, with an unwieldy centre section just over 60 ft from keel to deck containing tubes for three of the missiles. The hull also con-tained refrigerated storage for liquid oxygen, a liquid-oxygen production plant, kerosene storage and many other facilities. Fuelling could be done submerged, but the submarine would have to surface for a con-siderable period during and after the launch. The Jupiter was also expected to cause severe heat and blast damage as it slowly climbed out of its tube, even though huge ducts had to be provided to carry away the efflux.

Salvation came in the fairly assured prediction in 1956 that thermonuclear warheads could be made much lighter and more compact, and that use of ablative (heat-eroded) materials would make possible lighter re-entry vehicles to carry them safely back into the atmosphere and on to the target with satisfactory accuracy. Showing immense courage, and accepting unprecedented technical risk, Lockheed Missiles & Space Co. was formed to build a completely new submarine-launched weapon system based on a missile propelled by solid fuel, much smaller than Jupiter. This missile, Polaris (p.73) could be carried in greater quantity by a smaller submarine. It could be blown out of its launch tube before igniting its rocket propulsion, thus avoiding damage to the submarine. So attractive did the FBMS appear that a crash programme was begun to deploy it swiftly. The first Scorpion attack submarine was cut in two and completed with an extra 75 ft section housing a battery of sixteen Polaris missile tubes amidships, as well as a further large section for new navigation and control equipment and 10 ft for auxiliary machinery. Laid down as SSN 589 Scorpion on 1 November 1957, this vessel was launched on 9 June 1959 as the 130 ft-longer SSBN 598 George Washington, certainly the most notable and portentous naval vessel since the battleship Dreadnought of 1906. She commissioned on 30 December 1960, fully equipped with an operating missile system which had previously been developed with underwater launch tests off San Clemente, Calif., and with the complete navigation, fire control and missile launch system aboard the surface ship USS Observation Island. On 20 July 1960 George Washington fired a Polaris down the Atlantic Missile Range whilst submerged off the Florida coast. Less than three hours later she fired a second. Both impacted in the target area.

Political and military impact of this achievement was stunning. This submarine had a purpose totally different from that of all previous submarines, or any other kind of naval vessel. It had nothing to do with enemy naval power at all, but with the globally annihilating power of thermonuclear weapons used against enemy heartlands. The submarine was used to carry the missiles partly as a 'first stage' propulsion for what was originally still a fairly limited-range missile, but chiefly in order that the missiles should remain completely covert and secure from enemy discovery or attack. Though the view was expressed that an FBMS submarine might be tailed by a hostile attack submarine from the very start of her patrol as she left port, in fact it was soon demonstrated that, in 1960, the missile submarine could expect to proceed almost silently and alone to her designated firing position near a potentially hostile shore and there lie almost totally undiscoverable. On her first patrol, begun on 15 November 1960, George Washington lay submerged more than 66 days; some later patrols lasted even longer. Because of this a two-crew scheme was adopted from the outset, each FBMS vessel having a Gold Crew and a Blue Crew which changed places after each patrol.

Following 598 came four more 382-ft George Washingtons hurried through by taking materials and labour from attack submarines;

these were named Patrick Henry, Theodore Roosevelt, Robert E. Lee and Abraham Lincoln. They were followed by five of the new Ethan Allen design specially planned as FBMS carriers: Ethan Allen, Sam Houston, Thomas A. Edison, John Marshall and Thomas Jefferson. Longer by almost 30 ft, these had improved deep-diving hulls, much better crew accommodation and many detail changes including elimination of one of the triplicated SINS (Ship's Inertial Navigation System) installations carried by the George Washington. Precise knowledge of missile launch position is clearly vital, and in all FBMS submarines it is assured by two or three SINS, constantly updated by Transit satellite data, astro fixes and radio-navaid (e.g. Loran and VLF Omega) fixes. Special communications, including a VLF radio link at well below periscope depth, enable vital messages at national command level to be passed to submarines on station. Though bigger than the George Washingtons, the Ethan Allens were if anything slightly faster because of their better fineness ratio and better streamlined missile compartment bulge. They also went to sea, in 1961–63, armed with the longer-ranged Polaris A-2 missile. The first submarine A-2 shot was fired by Ethan Allen on 23 October 1961, and the following 6 May in the UK Christmas Island Test Area (central Pacific) she conducted the first-ever live test shot of a US missile with thermonuclear warhead.

After George Washington had gone to sea and proved the FBMS concept fully, the Navy told Congress it planned a formidable force of forty-five FBMS submarines. At a cost of rather more than $100 million each, the Navy was authorised in 1961-64 to buy thirty-one of an improved design known as the Lafayette class: Layfayette, Alexander Hamilton, Andrew Jackson, John Adams, James Monroe, Nathan Hale, Woodrow Wilson, Henry Clay, Daniel Webster, James Madison, Tecumseh, Daniel Boone, John C. Calhoun, Ulysses S. Grant, Von Steuben, Casimir Pulaski, Stonewall Jackson, Sam Rayburn, Nathaniel Greene, Benjamin Franklin, Simon Bolivar, Kamehameha, George Bancroft, Lewis and Clark, James K. Polk, George C. Marshall, Henry L. Stimson, George Washington Carver, Francis Scott Key, Mariano G. Vallejo and Will Rogers. Even longer than the Ethan Allen type, these extremely refined vessels carry a larger complement and incorporate minor differences (Daniel Webster has a completely different tall bow with diving planes on the upper fairing). Benjamin Franklin and subsequent examples have important propulsion modifications, possibly including natural circulation reactors and turbo-electric drive, to minimize noise.

As originally built, the first eight Lafayettes were armed with the Polaris A-2 and the remainder with the A-3 (p.73). The first A-3 submarine shot was made by Andrew Jackson on 26 October

1963. Between 1964 and 1967 the five George Washingtons were refitted with the A-3 missile, the original Mk 80 compressed-air ejection system being removed and replaced by the Mk 84 gas/steam system and associated fire control. In the late 1960s the Ethan Allens and the Lafayettes Nos 4 to 8 were all likewise converted to the A-3 missile. Finally, the Lafayettes Nos 1, 2, 10 and those that followed were all converted in 1969–74 to carry and fire the larger and much more formidable Poseidon missile (p.72), with Mk 88 launch and fire-control system. Each ship was converted whilst the reactor was recharged with a new core giving energy adequate for at least 400,000 miles of steaming. First to complete Poseidon conversion was James Madison, which fired the first submarine-launched Poseidon on 3 August 1970 and departed on patrol on 31 March 1971. Poseidon will not be fitted to the Ethan Allen and George Washington vessels, which will be the first to be withdrawn from the FBMS force upon delivery of new Trident-armed vessels.

US Trident submarines (72/73)
Originally designated ULMS (Underwater Long-range Missile System), Trident is a natural successor to the Polaris A-1, A-2, A-3 and Poseidon. Considerably more powerful than the last-named, it grew out of the Poseidon improvement programme, and re-

sulted from Strat-X, a Pentagon study which furnished the conceptual basis for the Undersea Long-range Missile System (ULMS). Full design development was authorised in 1969, and on 14 September 1971 the Navy was directed to begin engineering development of ULMS-1 and a new submarine to carry it, to be ready in 1981. Within three months the programme was accelerated to 1978, and ULMS-1 planned for possible installation in rebuilt Polaris/Poseidon submarines.

In 1972 ULMS was named Trident (for the three prongs of the missile, submarine and refit capability), the three-tined spear of the Greek god Poseidon. In the same year the SALT I (strategic arms limitation treaty) agreement restricted US missile submarines to the existing force (forty-one, with 656 missiles), with the option of discarding the fifty-four ageing land-based Titan missiles and acquiring three more submarines with fifty-four missiles. This affected the number and design of the Trident submarines. Some ULMS missile studies had been too big to fit readily into a 33 ft Lafayette hull, and schemes had been prepared for carriage in horizontal compartments outside the hull. Eventually Trident I, missile UGM-93A, was made similar in size to Poseidon, and the Trident submarine was designed by Electric Boat to have twenty-four launch tubes using the proven gas/steam expulsion system. Work also began in 1972 on a Trident II with a longer range. In

1973 a site was chosen for the Trident support and training base at Bangor, Washington, but there were environmental protests and deeper problems due to inflation, which began to eat into the number of new submarines and the retrofit programme.

As this book went to press the programme envisaged ten new Trident submarines, funded at the rate of one or two (alternately) each year to 1980. Electric Boat and Newport News will make the vessels, the first being ready in 1979. By far the biggest undersea craft in history, they will be faster, quieter and longer-ranged than any previous submarines and will be independent of bases outside the United States. The greater range of their missiles (4,000 miles) 'will allow them to remain within striking distance of potential targets from millions of additional square miles of ocean.' Their launch tubes will be large enough to permit 'substantial missile growth', fitting them for the bigger Trident II missile in the 1980s. Trident II will probably not be compatible with existing Polaris/Poseidon submarines, which will in any case then be coming to the end of their service life. On present plans the US Navy will retain twenty-five Lafayette-class, progressively re-armed with the Trident I system, adding 464 missiles to the 240 deployed in the ten new vessels for a total FBMS force of thirty-nine submarines carrying 704 missiles—six short of the permitted total. This compares with a proposed Soviet force of sixty-two submarines armed with 960 missiles.

US Advanced Attack Submarines

In 1964 a 'one-off' vessel, SSN 671, was authorised to test a radically improved reactor 'boiler', the Natural Circulation Reactor. In the original PWR the cooling liquid is circulated by large pumps, but in the NCR it is kept flowing by natural convection, the hot water in the reactor flowing out at the top under pressure from denser colder water coming in below. Developed by the Knolls Laboratory and built by General Electric as the S5G, the new reactor was first tested in a land prototype system, reaching criticality in September 1965. The submarine was launched in September 1967 as USS Narwhal, and was commissioned on 12 July 1969. She was appreciably larger than any previous attack submarine, and her beam of 38 ft seems to be an all-time record. As the S5G and its turbine plant gives more power than the standard S5 system, Narwhal is at least as fast. Operationally she resembles a Sturgeon.

Curiously, though Narwhal has this quieter, more reliable and simpler propulsion system, she retains a steam-turbine final drive. To provide an additional vehicle for exploration of quieter propulsion systems the US Navy finally managed to acquire SSN 685, named Glenard P. Lipscombe at its launch in June 1973. This is again an enlarged Sturgeon, though

157

retaining the standard basic reactor with modifications requiring the designation S5WA. The steam turbine drives a generator supplying an electric motor on the propeller shaft as in the earlier Tullibee. Quietness makes it easier for the submarine to listen for the enemy and harder for the enemy to detect in return. Lipscombe was commissioned in June 1974 and has proved to meet initial requirements. She will serve several uses in research programmes involving many kinds of hardware, whilst being immediately capable of operations.

Some of the lessons learned with these two experimental attack submarines have been incorporated in the new standard attack class named for the lead-ship USS Los Angeles, SSN 688. By 1975 23 units of the class had been authorised, and it is significant that all appear likely to be built by the 'good' performers in the earlier programmes: Electric Boat and Newport News yard. Though impressive vessels, much bigger than any previous attack submarines, and powered by a reactor/turbine system giving about twice the power used previously, the Los Angeles class have run into Congressional trouble on grounds of cost/effectiveness. A critic could claim they cost twice as much as a Sturgeon, i.e. about $220 million each, yet cannot do a bigger or better job. As I write there are indications the class may not extend beyond SSN 710 and that smaller attack submarines with different features will follow.

British Explorer and Excalibur

So nearly did the U-boat come to bringing Britain to its knees in World War 2 that the Admiralty were justifiably sensitive to any new improvement in its capability. The discovery at the end of the war of the radical new propulsion system of the Type XVIIB and similar designs naturally triggered a development programme in Britain. (As described earlier, U1407 was salvaged and, after years of delay, commissioned as HMS Meteorite.) But as the war had already been won, a lot of the steam went out of the project, in quite a literal sense. Instead of frantically working to stay ahead, or get ahead, as was being done in the United States and Soviet Union, a leisurely pace was adopted in an environment of extreme financial stringency, the post-war government doing all it could to reduce defence expenditure even at the expense of future weakness.

Despite the fact that the machinery was derived directly from German designs, the first of two experimental HTP (high-test peroxide) submarines, HMS Explorer, did not begin her trials until 1957. She proved to be impressively fast, and ten years earlier might have proved useful. As it was, she emerged into the new world of the nuclear submarine, which had started later and been carried to fruition much faster. Moreover, despite the considerable development background of German work, HTP technology proved difficult to the point of being dangerous, so that one RN submariner said 'I think the best thing we can do with peroxide is try to get it adopted by potential enemies.' Neither Explorer nor her near-sister Excalibur had much contribution to make in these circumstances, and they were scrapped in 1969–70.

British Porpoise and Oberon classes (74)

Designed in the early 1950s to an extremely high standard, making the fullest use of every development in World War 2 and later, these were the last classes of British conventional submarine. They are outstanding vessels in every respect, and have an enviable reputation for performance and efficiency. Their all-welded hulls are stressed for diving deeper than any previous RN submarines, and were at one time unique in that, except in Orpheus, the superstructure above the hull is largely of glass-reinforced plastics to reduce weight. Hydrodynamically they were the most streamlined submarines of their day, having greater beam than the A-class and a very clean hull with a slender but lofty sail in place of an old-fashioned conning tower. They have never carried a gun.

Both classes are propelled by two diesel-electric sets, the Admiralty Standard Range 16-cylinder diesels being used to drive the generators to supply the propulsion motors on the surface or charge the batteries while submerged. The stored electrical capacity, using a new kind of cell, exceeds that in any other British submarines. Likewise the electric propulsion motors are of high power (5,000 h.p. in Porpoise-class, 6,000 h.p. in Oberons), giving an underwater speed almost as high as in the peroxide boats. Electric drive minimizes noise, and the absence of exterior excrescences is self-evident. Interior living conditions are much better than in the A-class (the previous best), with air-conditioning for Arctic or tropical waters, oxygen replenishment and carbon monoxide elimination and fresh water distilled from the sea. These submarines can remain submerged for as long as six weeks, and can stay down for several days without using the snort (Schnorkel). Both classes carry a large torpedo reload capacity, with three types of torpedo, and have very efficient sonar and high-definition radar (the latter being used chiefly for navigation in confined waters or poor visibility).

With their remarkable silence and outstanding efficiency these submarines will continue in service for many years. The Porpoise class comprises: Porpoise, Rorqual, Grampus, Narwhal, Cachalot, Finwhale, Walrus and Sealion. Oberons are as follows: Orpheus (the first, with light-alloy superstructure), Oberon, Odin, Olympus, Onslaught, Otter, Oracle, Otus, Osiris, Ocelot, Opossum, Opportune, Ojibwa (Royal Canadian Navy) and Onyx.

HMS Dreadnought

Ninth Royal Naval vessel to bear this name, Dreadnought was conceived in 1952 as the Royal Navy's first nuclear submarine. Project studies continued at high priority but at a low and controversial rate, the main trouble being the much faster progress in the United States in this revolutionary field. At an early date—about 1954—the decision was taken to adopt the teardrop hull form proven by USS Albacore. Much later, probably in 1956, it was finally decided that, instead of going ahead with an all-British nuclear vessel, much time and money would be saved by accepting the American lead and cashing in on US nuclear technology. Dreadnought thus has an American propulsion system. At the same time, Rolls-Royce and Associates, which had been collaborating with the UK Atomic Energy Authority in the development of a completely new nuclear propulsion system for submarines—a task for which the UKAEA gas-cooled reactor was unsuitable—was instructed to continue to develop a British nuclear drive, but now with the collaboration of Westinghouse and the US Navy.

Launched on Trafalgar Day (21 October) 1960, Dreadnought is far from being a mere research vessel. In most essentials of hull and propulsion she resembles a US Navy Skipjack, but her front half is entirely British and at the time of her commissioning probably made her the most formidable attack submarine in the world. The upper part of the bulged bow is modified in profile to suit the needs of what can be assumed to be a sonar array of exceptional power and discrimination, with 'windows' extending

around the 'forehead' of the ship. Below this installation are the six tubes, behind which is a large magazine for reloading several times. Further aft are crew facilities unprecedented even in surface vessels, though in this respect Dreadnought merely followed what had become standard nuclear-submarine practice in the US Navy. Apart from hull-cracking, she proved to be popular and reliable, and in 1970 completed a major refit in the course of which her nuclear core was refuelled and her ballast-tank valves were changed to reduce noise.

British Valiant, Churchill and Swiftsure classes (75/76/77)

Derived directly from HMS Dreadnought, all but one of these fine submarines was built by Vickers at Barrow, all being ordered in 1960–72 and completed in 1966–76. They are deep-diving high-speed attack submarines, officially classed as Fleet Submarines and for the first time fully capable of realising all the aims of the high-performance submarine capable of keeping up with a surface fleet. It is, however, unlikely that the extremely costly and comprehensively equipped members of this class will ever be seen in close formation with surface ships in normal exercises or in actual operations. Their task is to hunt down their prey alone, without risk of being attacked by friendly forces, and as they are nuclear they may be expected to spend very little time on the surface.

Rolls-Royce and Associates designed the pressurised water reactor (PWR) along Westinghouse lines, and the entire propulsion system was made and developed in Britain, at first with the help of a shore prototype at the Admiralty Reactor Test Establishment at Dounreay. The hulls are generally similar to that of Dreadnought but rather larger, though the third group (Swiftsure class) have markedly different design and have only five tubes and a smaller crew. Completion of the first group—Valiant and Warspite—was held back to speed work on the Resolution-class missile submarines. As Resolution was launched she was followed on the slipway by the first of the next group, comprising Churchill, Conqueror and Courageous.

The third group, incorporating major improvements, comprises Swiftsure, Sovereign, Superb and Sceptre, plus one as yet un-named. It has been stated that these submarines have sonar gear (in the expected 'forehead' position) to detect at much greater ranges than that fitted in British patrol submarines. They can operate at greater depth than any previous Royal Navy submarine (in excess of 1,000 ft) and were the first ships to be equipped with the new British Mk 24 homing torpedo. As early as April 1967 Valiant ran 12,000 miles (19,400 km) submerged from Singapore to Britain in 28 days, and month-long submerged voyages have since become routine.

British Polaris submarines

The swift development of the sub-marine-launched Polaris ballistic missile by Lockheed and the US Navy reverberated around the world. The US State Department pushed the idea of a NATO multi-national force of surface ships carrying these missiles, while the British talked about various 'poor man's Polaris' schemes with shorter range that might be launched from small conventional submarines. In December 1962, approximately seven years after the British government learned of the Polaris programme, Prime Minister Macmillan was at last advised that it was a desirable weapon for the Royal Navy, and he accordingly dropped the air-launched Skybolt and concluded a deal with President Kennedy for the purchase of Polaris A-3 missiles, without warheads, at a price carrying a 5 per cent. surcharge as a British contribution to research and development. Britain undertook to develop a warhead.

Four submarines were authorised in February 1963, laid down with maximum speed in pairs by Vickers (lead yard) and Cammell Laird; a fifth was announced in 1964 but was cancelled by a new government the following year. The vessels are: Resolution (S22), Repulse (S23), Renown (S26) and Revenge (S27). Though incorporating a 16-tube missile section generally similar to that of a Lafayette, the rest of these fine ships are all-British in concept. Obvious contrasts with the US FBMS lie in the accommodation, the six bow tubes and the hull-mounted planes. Cost averaged about £39 million each, or nearly £55 million including missiles and equipment. Further substantial sums were spent on a technical support and training centre at Faslane and on improved facilities elsewhere. Each vessel fired two missiles down the Atlantic Missile Range before going on operational patrol. All have now undergone refits, but no decision has been announced regarding conversion to fire Poseidon, with Mk 88 fire control. The four Royal Navy submarines are thus, at the moment, the only ships left still armed with any form of Polaris. Doubtless a decision to convert to Poseidon will be announced in time for this to be worth while, though the question of what to do when these ships reach the end of their active life is probably incapable of being answered at a time of weak national will and severe economic restraint. Certainly any plan to maintain the Royal Navy's deterrent effectiveness with Trident ships would appear incapable of fulfilment.

French attack classes (78/79)

Not unnaturally the French Navy based their first post-war class on the German Type XXI. Powered by 4,000 h.p. Schneider diesels, with 5,000 hp electric motors when submerged, the Narval class comprised six boats laid down in 1951–56 and commissioned in 1957–60. Names are Narval, Marsouin, Dauphin, Requin, Espadon and Morse. After ten years they were rebuilt with new conning towers, new equipment and SEMT-Piel-

stick diesels and two-shaft diesel-electric drive. They were followed by the Aréthuse class—Aréthuse, Argonaute, Amazone and Ariane—of small coastal 400-ton boats with four bow tubes and four reloads. These in turn were followed by the important Daphne class, smaller, lower-powered and slower than the Narvals, but fitted with no fewer than twelve tubes (eight bow, four stern). Daphne commissioned in 1964, followed by Diane, Doris, Eurydice, Flore, Galatée, Minerve, Junon, Venus, Psyche and Sirène by 1970. Minerve and Eurydice have been lost, and Sirène sunk but recovered. South Africa bought three Daphnes, Pakistan three and Portugal four, while Spain built four with French help.

French SNLE (80)

Standing for Sous-marins Nucléaires Lanceurs d'Engins (nuclear submarines for launching missiles), the SNLE class of five vessels are large and efficient and represent a fantastic achievement for French technology and industry. Like the Dassault-Breguet Mirage IVA supersonic bomber, they were built without foreign assistance to deliver the French nuclear deterrent, which was itself created almost entirely without external aid (indeed, in the teeth of American opposition). Unlike Britain, which decided not to build a fifth submarine for this purpose, the French have completed five and authorized a sixth, and thus will achieve the optimum balance between expenditure and round-the-year deterrence with two or more SNLEs always on station and ready to fire.

Like the other submarines in this category of the USA, Soviet Union, and Britain, the SNLE is a floating missile base. It does carry conventional torpedoes but these are normally regarded as defensive weapons and it would be extremely unlikely that such a costly monster would ever be used against other shipping. The main armament of sixteen MSBS missiles is all-important, and the submarine's task is to carry this formidable battery to a pre-selected location and lie there quietly awaiting orders to fire.

All five of the SNLE vessels were built at the Direction des Constructions et Armes Navales de Cherbourg, whose Slipway 3—from which have come nineteen submarines since 1922—is amply long and high enough even for these giants, and equipped also with an adjacent prefabrication plant and mechanical handling installations for loads of up to 260 tons. Each SNLE hull is made up of a bow and stern and twenty-four intermediate prefabricated sections each weighing up to 200 tons. Assembly required more than 200 highly qualified welders, who used approximately 60 tons of welding rod on each hull, all of it deposited with extreme precision. The resulting hulls are easily the largest ever built, except for the Soviet Delta and Yankee classes which are almost identical in size.

Though details of the propulsion system are classified it is known to be a pressurized water reactor fuelled with highly enriched uranium. Design and development was handled by the Département Propulsion Nucléaire (DPN) of the Commissariat à l'Energie Atomique with manufacturing development by the ECAN d'Indret. The prototype propulsion system was tested at Cadarache. Nuclear fuel is supplied by the enriched-uranium factory at Pierrelatte. Diagrams of SNLE propulsion all show various circulating pumps, including one for the primary circuit conveying heat from the reactor to the main heat exchanger. This is a noisy item, and in the nuclear attack submarine to be laid down in 1976 the American system of natural convectional circulation will probably be used instead.

Steam from the reactor drives the main propulsion turbine and also a turbo-alternator serving the electrical needs of the vessel. An emergency d.c. electric motor is inserted in the final propeller-shaft drive, and in the event of any interruption in steam generation or turbine failure can be connected to storage batteries for low-speed propulsion over distances greater than 5,575 miles.

The heart of the SNLE is the CTD (Centre de Traitement des Données), the data processing centre where all numerical information on board is handled by four digital computers. The four primary tasks of the CTD are: control of MSBS targeting, trajectory calculation and launch control; presentation of the complete local tactical situation in the form of bright displays and readouts, using information from all the on-board sensors; navigation, using the inertial platform with intermittent updating by the astro-view periscope; and direction of torpedo firings. The need to handle many types of calculation simultaneously, and to control numerous systems in real time, called for a very advanced and elaborate computer installation with over 300 km (190 miles) of cable and 250,000 junctions. Naturally these large submarines have the most complete installation of navigation, communications and sensing systems, with radar, ECM, active and passive sonars for both surveillance and attack, passive listening systems, acoustic telemetry and various sounding devices for the seabed and surface.

An all-French missile, including the warhead, MSBS is carried in sixteen vertical launch tubes in the same configuration as the pioneer US Navy FBMS submarines. The missile itself is illustrated on p.79 in its original form. Defensive armament comprises four bow tubes for homing torpedoes, probably of the L3 Alcatel acoustic type with diameter of 550 mm (21·65 in.). A total of eighteen torpedoes are carried.

The first SNLE was named Le Redoutable, and was launched in the presence of the French President, Gen. de Gaulle, on 29 March 1967. On 2 July 1969 she began sea trials, operating from the SNLE base at the Ile Longue near Brest, where are located the SNLE and MSBS training schools, storage,

maintenance and operational command facilities. The French Navy emphasized the outstanding success of the trials programme with this first SNLE. In 5,000 hours of reactor criticality, during which time she steamed 10,000 miles, she made more than twenty missile launch tests, some in salvoes of up to four. The second, Le Terrible, was launched on 12 December 1969, and delivered for test on 16 July 1971. After very successful trials she spent some months at Cherbourg being readied for operations and returned as an operational vessel to Ile Longue in March 1972. The third SNLE is Le Foudroyant, laid down on the same No 3 slipway in December 1969, launched on 4 December 1971 and delivered for test during the summer of 1973. The fourth submarine is l'Indomptable, laid down in January 1972, launched on 17 September 1974 and due to begin sea trials in early 1976. Fifth is Le Tonnant, laid down in the winter 1974–75 after launch of l'Indomptable, and due to commission in 1978. The sixth, l'Inflexible, was to be laid down in 1976.

French Agosta (81)

The first vessel named after the great sea battle of Agosta (Sicily), fought between France and Holland on 22 April 1676, was a high-speed submarine of the main inter-war class (p.34). The present Agosta continues the tradition, being the first of four high-speed attack submarines with conventional propulsion ordered under the 3rd Plan Militaire in June 1971. All four are being built by the Direction des Constructions et Armes Navales de Cherbourg, Agosta being the eightieth submarine constructed at that historic yard.

Hulls are assembled from fourteen prefabricated sections, each weighing about 35 tons, with special closures at front and rear. A new steel is being used with excellent elasticity and welding characteristics, and all welds are subject to extremely precise control. Propulsion is by main and cruising electric motors fed by 320 lead/acid cells recharged by an 850 kW Pielstick diesel generator. Thanks to the installed power and advanced hull form, these are probably the fastest conventionally propelled submarines in the world. It should be noted that the schnorkel-equipped diesel never drives the screw direct, but always recharges the batteries. The French Navy is especially pleased with the degree of automaticity throughout these modern submarines, with instant control of trajectory, internal atmosphere and all dynamic systems.

Details of the weaponry remain classified, but navigation and detection systems are very comprehensive. Basically there are two sonars, groupings of microphones for passive listening, acoustic telemetry systems, sounders, cavitation detectors and various sound and electromagnetic signature systems. From the sail protrude surveillance and attack periscopes, various radar aerials and radio and countermeasures aerials. In the bows are the four 550 mm (21·65 in.) tubes, the total number of torpedoes being twenty, handled by fully mechanised loading systems for repeated firing under water at short intervals.

Agosta was laid down in November 1972, launched on 19 October 1974 and began sea trials in October 1975. Beveziers was laid down in May 1973, was launched in the spring of 1975 and was to commission in 1976. La Praya and Ouessant are respectively timed about 9 and 18 months later. In addition to these four vessels the Spanish Navy is building two more of this class with the assistance of the French Direction Technique des Constructions Navales, and in June 1975 three were ordered from France by the Republic of South Africa.

Swedish Sjöormen class (82)

Since World War 2 the Royal Swedish Navy has equipped itself with successive classes of small but effective submarines, built at Kockums yard at Malmo and the Royal Swedish Dockyard at Karlskrona. The Draken class of 1961–62 were the last to have the traditional hull form. The Sjöormen (Sea Serpent) design introduced a modern fat but short profile, with circular pressure hull (no deck casing) giving much greater displacement while cutting length by one-quarter. Sjöormen was launched in January 1967 and completed in July of that year. She was followed by Sjölejonet, Sjöhunden, Sjöhasten and

Sjöbjörnen, all completed by 1969. They are quiet, despite their submerged speed of 20 knots, the large five-blade propeller being electrically driven. Five fractionally bigger submarines are now in the final stages of construction.

Soviet submarines

After the 1917 revolution the Red Navy took a very long time to find its feet. The first submarines were based on old British (L-class) or Italian designs, but eventually a considerable number (possibly as many as 80) were built of a 600-ton patrol type known as the Shch class (from Shchuka=Pike, the lead ship), and these saw a lot of service during World War 2. Another important group were the S (Stalinets) class, derived from the German Type IA (Turkish Gür) design which was given to the Russians in return for their help in getting German U-boat construction off the ground in the early 1930s. By far the most numerous of all Soviet submarines in World War 2 were the tiny Malyutka (=small) classes, of which possibly as many as 200 were built between 1928 and 1944. These grew from the 180-ton size to a more practical 300–350 tons in the final series (XII to XV). It was mainly because of the M classes that Soviet submarine construction in the 1930s far outnumbered that of other nations. No reliable figures have ever been published, but the total for 1930–39 of all classes probably exceeded 220 (Italy, the second biggest builder, completed 89). The M classes (**90/91**) were prefabricated, and shipped overland, or by canal, for assembly. The number of sections grew from four (M VI) to six (M VII–XIV) and finally to seven, because of the growth of these boats. The only other series built in numbers were the big K (Katyusha) class, fast cruiser boats of 1,390 tons with ten tubes. Little has been revealed of Soviet submarine activity during World War 2; the Red Navy made little attempt to collaborate with the other Allied fleets.

Soviet W (Whisky) class (84)*

After World War 2 the Soviet Navy made the maximum use of information gained from its former allies, and even greater use of captured German submarines, plans and engineers. Several experimental submarines were tested, at least one having HTP (peroxide) propulsion, but none led to a production class. Despite the obvious attractions of such new propulsion technology the final choice was a new standard design of patrol submarine of completely conventional type, closely comparable with the British A class of the late war years but fitted with more powerful electric motors for higher underwater speed. The design had been started early in the war but repeatedly delayed after 1945 to take in new technology.

---

* Modern Soviet submarines are known by class-letters and, in NATO, by that letter's phonetic name, e.g. W=Whisky.

Design was completed by 1950, and plans were laid for mass-production on a stupendous scale. This was at the time the Stalin regime was trying to build a giant navy along conventional lines, and by using rapid assembly (often on floating docks) of factory-built prefabricated parts it was calculated 800 could be built in nine years. Lead yard was Sormovo at Gorkiy, on the Volga, part-finished submarines being towed by river and canal for fitting out at other centres. Biggest production came from the giant yard at Severodvinsk (formerly Molotovsk). After Stalin's death production was cut back, and it fell to zero in about 1956 by which time the total was at least 200 and probably 276—a colossal fleet, and greater than any save the U-boat VIIC. Whisky submarines entered service from early 1952 with all the Soviet fleets, and from 1957 they began to be sold or transferred in increasing numbers to friendly nations.

There is nothing remarkable about the Whisky design itself, which was deliberately based on established principles to ensure low cost, trouble-free service and predictable performance. By the standards of 1950 it was adequate, and perhaps the most remarkable feature of this huge force was how little the design changed and how nearly identical all W class submarines are to each other (apart from the 'Canvas Bag' group, described later). The only major change was the deletion of the twin 57 mm (2·24 in.) guns, sometimes augmented by a 3·9 in. aft of the conning tower, fitted in early examples. Probably the torpedo tubes can carry and fire the German type of torpedo mine; no special Soviet minelaying submarines have been seen. Their speed was quite good for their day, but while still in production they were being outclassed by the teardrop hull and nuclear propulsion, and a more serious failing was their considerable noise. From the mid-1960s Whiskys began to be withdrawn from active use. The number tied up inactive has been increasing considerably, and in the mid-1970s the force is down to about 100 and diminishing at the rate of about twenty each year. With withdrawals accelerating, the whole group will probably have gone from Soviet fleets by 1978, but leaving behind a massive force of experienced crews putting their skills to use in later submarines

About sixty of these submarines were either sold new to other countries, built under licence or transferred from Soviet strength. The biggest foreign group is a fleet of at least twenty-one constructed in Chinese yards between 1956–64, initially from prefabricated sections supplied by sea from the Soviet Union. In 1975 all twenty-one appeared still to be in active commission. Examples of W class vessels transferred from the Soviet Navy are the four named Orzel (292), Sokol (293), Kondor (294) and Bielik (295) of the Polish Navy (which had six, but sold two in 1959 to Indonesia), and Pobeda and

Slava of Bulgaria. Two were transferred to Albania in 1960, and the Albanians seized two from Soviet forces leaving Albania in 1961. Four were freely supplied to North Korea, though not all these are in active use. At least six were sold to Egypt in 1957–62, apparently in new condition, and in 1966 two were returned and replaced by two of the improved R class; additional Egyptian Whiskys have since sailed to Leningrad for refit (or possible disposal). Biggest purchaser of Whiskys was Indonesia, which between 1959–62 bought fourteen (two of them from Poland). Names of surviving Indonesian submarines are Trisula (402), Nagabanda (403), Nagarangsang (404), Hendrajala (405), Alugoro (406), Tjandrasa (408), Widjajadanu (409), Pasopati (410), Tjundmani (411) and Bramastra (412); the two ex-Polish vessels have been withdrawn and the force has been run down to five or six in active commission.

Soviet Whisky Canvas Bag class (84)

In 1959–63 at least five W class submarines were rebuilt as radar pickets. Though retaining their torpedo tubes, their prime function is long-range sea/sky surveillance using a large S or L band radar which has the NATO code name Boat Sail. The horizontal parabolic reflector both rotates and oscillates in azimuth on a large pillar mount at the rear of the completely new sail (fin). The name Canvas Bag was prompted by the fabric cover which was originally used to hide the radar aerial except when the equipment was actually in use, presumably for security reasons.

Soviet Whisky Twin Cylinder class (84/85/93)

Existence of the huge force of Whisky submarines, which was becoming surplus to requirements even while most of the boats were still new, led to several being converted for fresh tasks. The first such conversion to enter operational service was the Twin Cylinder, for firing the long-range cruise missile known to NATO as Shaddock, and also called SS-N-3. This missile has been very widely used from both land and sea platforms and certainly exists in numerous different forms; unfortunately it has hardly ever been seen outside its opaque tube launcher. It is launched from the inclined tube under the thrust of two large solid boosters. Cruise propulsion is provided by an integral ramjet, with lift from flick-out hinged wings. The missile is roll-stabilized, carries a large conventional or nuclear warhead and has over-the-horizon range of from 200–320 miles (extreme limits) depending on sub-type, cruising at an estimated Mach 1·5. In installations on surface vessels line-of-sight target range and bearing, and at least initial guidance, is provided by a distinctive radar, known to NATO as Scoop Net, with upper and lower roll-stabilized aerials and various provisions for ECM, IFF and clutter rejection. No such radar is installed on the W Twin Cylinder submarines, and in view of the obvious limitations of these vessels it is likely that they are for Shaddock trials and training and are not regarded as operational.

Each submarine carries two missile cylinders on the deck immediately abaft the fin. The latter incorporates a prominent rear tower which is nevertheless too small to carry a Scoop Net radar. From this a companion way leads down to the 'breech' of the two cylinders. The latter differ considerably from those carried by Soviet surface ships, and more closely resemble those of the mobile vehicle used to fire the Shaddock coast-defence land version. Each cylinder is fixed in azimuth, so the whole submarine must be pointed stern-on in the direction of the target. The cylinders are linked together, and elevate as one unit to the firing angle of about 18 deg. The cylinders are probably watertight, and when loaded probably prohibit deep diving. For firing, the submarine must surface, and the muzzle covers are opened manually with the cylinders horizontal. A large breakwater dam around the entire front (i.e. breech) end of the cylinders protects personnel on deck from rough seas. When the missiles are fired the breech closures are almost certainly open to reduce recoil and permit the swift dispersal of hot rocket gas. The biggest puzzle is how the missiles are guided in flight. Several sources have suggested mid-course guidance is effected by aircraft radio command and that the missile has infra-red terminal homing, but

neither seems especially plausible. What is probable is that the submarine installations have a shorter range than those of surface vessels.

Soviet Whisky Long Bin class (83)

No submarine designer could rest content with the Twin Cylinder installation, which was not only a primitive lash-up but also must have resulted in the noisiest submarine of modern times (except when proceeding at a snail's pace). The important Shaddock missile clearly demanded a more extensive conversion of the W class submarines, and the next installation revealed a complete rebuild of the mid-section. The existing fin was removed, the hull cut in two, a section about 25 ft long added to increase displacement, and a completely new and much larger superstructure added. Inside this are launch cylinders for four missiles.

The cylinders are carried side-by-side in left and right pairs. All are fixed at the correct launch angle, which in this case appears to be about 15 deg. but unlike Twin Cylinder they point forward. Before firing, each cylinder is covered by a watertight muzzle closure and in this installation it is possible that deep diving is permitted with missiles loaded. Underwater performance is likely to be much better than that of Twin Cylinder, though probably slightly degraded in comparison with the original W class. Though less noisy than Twin Cylinder, the Long Bin submarines are nevertheless known to be far from quiet and to be relatively easy to distinguish by acoustic means. For launching, the submarine is surfaced, pointed at the distant target with the chosen cylinder opened, and the missile fired. Means is almost certain to be provided for rapid escape of rocket gas, though in this installation there is probably significant recoil effect as the large weapon is fired. Again, there is no evidence of Scoop Net or any other missile guidance system, and NATO observers have come to the conclusion that, irrespective of whether or not Shaddock has any form of homing, there must be some form of mid-course guidance by radio command from some other platform such as a radar-equipped aircraft.

Soviet Romeo class   (88)
The immediate successors of the huge W class, the R class (Romeo) are conventional patrol submarines with more modern features. Compared with the W, the hull is longer and wider, though draught is actually slightly reduced. On it is mounted a more slender fin, with tall central conning tower; unlike the W class this fin was never designed to carry guns. In the bows is a sonar installation much more advanced and efficient than the vulnerable keel installation of W class vessels, and considerable efforts have clearly been made to reduce underwater noise. Production in the Soviet Union began in about 1957 but stopped within

three years, after only fourteen had been delivered, as a result of the rapid development of submarine technology. Between 1966–69 six were sold or given to the Egyptian Navy.

More significantly, perhaps, plans of the Romeo were supplied to China shortly before the break with the Soviet Union in 1960. Possibly some prefabricated parts or complete submarines were also supplied. By 1970 the Chinese were building three or four of this type at Lü-Ta annually, and by 1975 their force was thought to number more than twenty.

Soviet Quebec class   (86/87)
The only small coastal submarines in Soviet service, these vessels are thought to have stemmed from one of the post-war research submarines built with HTP propulsion. This is because they have three shafts (screws) and in the early examples some form of closed-cycle propulsion was fitted on at least one shaft. Today they seem to be ordinary diesel-electric boats, with quite a clean exterior and fair performance, though they carry only four tubes. Altogether twenty-two were delivered in 1954–57, thirteen of these being built by Sudomekh Yard at Leningrad.

Soviet Zulu class   (86/87/89)
Bearing numerous traces of German influence, and probably designed with German assistance in the early post-war years, these were the first large patrol submarines to be built in the Soviet Union after 1945

and have had a successful career over the past twenty years. Long and quite streamlined, and closely related to the earlier W class, they have conventional diesel-electric propulsion with three sets of machinery on three shafts. Thanks to their size they have very long range, and their original armament comprised six bow tubes and four at the stern (they originally had two 25 mm guns). Altogether about thirty-five are known to have been delivered, from Sudomekh and Severodvinsk in 1951–55. There are at least four different types of conning-tower fin, several of this class having been rebuilt with either of two types of much enlarged fin presumably accommodating additional sensing equipment.

In recent years several Zulus have been active in the Mediterranean, though they are probably now used as operational training submarines. In 1955–57 at least seven were withdrawn from service and rebuilt, reportedly at the Zhdanov (Leningrad) yard, as the world's first ballistic-missile submarines. The missile was the SS-N-4 Sark solid-propellant weapon, which is generally thought to have been a research and development vehicle to explore the problems of the submarine/missile system. The converted submarines are code-named Zulu V (the final sub-type of Zulu patrol submarine having been Zulu IV), and they incorporated a 36 ft extra section of hull spliced in amidships. On top was a considerably extended fin incorporating vertical launch tubes for two Sarks, which were too large to fit vertically inside the hull. By the mid-1960s the Zulu Vs had begun to be withdrawn, and only two remained in 1975, used for various duties unconnected with missiles.

Soviet Foxtrot class (90/91)

These fine conventionally propelled patrol submarines formed a natural follow-on to the Zulus (though the NATO code-name did not; from this point on, the West adopted a policy of more or less random designations). The F class hull is almost identical to that of the lengthened Zulu V, though cleaned up in detail. In the bows is a sonar installation of an advanced type, apparently the same as that of the smaller R class though with the top projection (probably an underwater telephone) mounted further aft. The fin is not over-large and quite streamlined, and appears to be generally to a common design in all the fifty-six vessels of this type known to have entered service. There are three shafts, as in the Zulus, with diesel-electric propulsion on each. Curiously, though the diesel power has been reduced to 6,000 h.p., and the electric final drive increased in power to the same amount, speeds appear to be almost the same as those of the Zulu class; surface performance is thought to be somewhat higher. With the Golf class, the Foxtrots were built after the development of a submarine nuclear propulsion system, showing that the Soviet

Union had no wish to economise on defence spending and was prepared to build large numbers of conventional submarines to reach chosen levels of force.

It is universally agreed that these have proved extremely successful submarines. It is likely that the three sets of diesel-electric propulsion were standardised as the type of conventional drive for all non-nuclear submarines. The propulsion is markedly quieter than that in W or Z class vessels, and appears to have been very reliable. At the same time there cannot be a great deal of very advanced technology in these submarines, because in 1967 the transfer or sale of four to the Indian Navy was agreed, and the Indian submarines—named Kalvari, Kanderi, Karanj and Kursura—arrived at Bombay between July 1968 and April 1970. Since 1965 Foxtrots have been the most numerous class of Soviet submarine in the Mediterranean, and they are encountered all over the world.

Soviet Golf class (92)
This was the first class of ballistic-missile submarine in the world to enter operational service. The hull is derived from that of the F class but is significantly larger, to carry the biggest fin ever fitted to production submarines. This fin was designed 'from a clean sheet of paper' to carry and fire three ballistic missiles, drawing upon the experience gained with the Zulu V conversions. Initially the only missile available was Sark, and it was around this that the design was

tailored. The three tubes are vertical and in line, each having its own inner watertight closure and hinged top hatch which opens to the left (port). In view of the early timing of Sark it is likely that some form of radio guidance was needed by this missile, and this must be provided by equipment on board the submarine. There appears to be ample space for radio and radar in the fin, and an early sonar installation is to be seen in the bows. Propulsion is by the same triple diesel-electric installation as in the F class.

The number of G class submarines is at least twenty-two. They were built at Severodvinsk and Komsomolsk and commissioned in 1958–61. Like the Zulu V trials vessels the Gs have to surface to fire their missiles, and they then present enormous radar targets from abeam. When the much improved Serb (SS-N-5) missile became available in 1963, with underwater-launch capability, it was progressively introduced in place of Sark. As the much more costly H class (described later) were dealt with first, it was 1966–67 before conversions started on the Gs. As a result they were judged not all worth converting, and in the mid-1970s about half were equipped to fire Serb, being restyled in the West Golf II or G2. The rest are designated Golf I or G1. It is doubtful that they will remain operational much longer, but have certainly been used for ballistic-missile training. In 1959 plans were supplied to China, and in 1964 one vessel of this class was completed at Dairen. China has no Sark or Serb missiles, and has since 1960 been cut off from Soviet technical help, but it is likely that at least one of the classes of Chinese-developed missile is tailored to this type of submarine.

Soviet November class

As the United States began its development of a submarine pro-propulsion system using nuclear power in 1949 it was only to be expected that the relevant information would not be long delayed in reaching the Soviet Union. In the event the time interval was about four years, and though details are lacking it seems certain that the technology adopted in the Soviet Union follows closely that practised by the US Navy, AEC and Westinghouse, with enriched uranium in a pressurised water reactor. Once developed and run, in 1956, this propulsion system appears to have been standardised for all subsequent Soviet nuclear submarines, though the reactor heat-exchange system and turbines are rated at two power levels, 22,500 and 24,000 s.h.p. In the first nuclear class, the N (November), the lower rating was adopted. It was amply sufficient, even though these were easily the largest Soviet submarines constructed at that time. The advantage of following the United States in nuclear propulsion technology is highlighted by the fact that this class was not preceded by a research prototype.

In view of the sustained high power, the hull form was made more streamlined and akin to the teardrop in form, and the fin was held to the minimum. At the same time, the deck casing was provided with a continuous row of free-flood perforations which inevitably generate turbulence and noise in underwater running (early Novembers also had noisy propulsion). Another rather interesting decision was the installation of four of the small 400 mm (15·75 in.) short-range homing torpedoes in the stern. This quad installation has since become the standard armament for use against other submarines, though all the visible sonar equipment in Soviet submarines is now in the bow. It is not clear exactly how these aft-pointing small tubes are used.

In the West the N class are regarded as 'fleet submarines', though there is no evidence that they are meant to proceed in close company with surface forces. As nuclear vessels they are free-ranging over the entire globe, and as the first in Soviet hands have certainly been used for valuable detailed navigation in places where no Soviet vessel had previously been. Yet their design was only an interim one, and construction was held to fourteen, the last being commissioned in 1963. One was lost southwest of the British Isles in 1970.

Soviet Echo class (94)

Representing an unusual class of missile platforms in which nuclear propulsion is used for limitless endurance rather than high speed, the E series were the natural successors to the unsatisfactory Whisky Long Bin as the carriers of the Shaddock cruise missile. Compared with the earlier vessels they are much larger, and were at the time of their introduction by far the biggest submarines in the world apart from the early Polaris vessels. Classed as Cruise Missile Submarines, they are global cruisers carrying a weapon used only against cities or the largest hostile warships. It is worth noting that the Shaddock is a winged vehicle much easier to intercept than a ballistic missile, and because of its flat trajectory and longer time of flight, and probable need for evasive action, poses more severe guidance problems which are considered to require external assistance during flight. It also requires the submarine to surface before firing. The US Navy abandoned cruise missiles in 1957, putting all subsequent effort into the FBMS, yet in the Soviet Union the Shaddock has been deployed extremely widely aboard surface vessels and this important class of submarines, as well as the smaller Juliet class.

As in the Juliets, the missiles are contained in launch cylinders normally enclosed within the high deck casing. Each cylinder is individually hinged at the rear and can be hydraulically elevated to the firing position, the rear end moving back into a large cutout in the casing. A total of six missiles was at first installed, in three pairs, all firing forwards and capable of being launched individually or in a quickly rippled salvo. The hull was made appreciably longer than that of the nuclear N class, though of slightly narrower beam, and is similar to that of the earlier H class. The same propulsion system was used, and the same armament of large bow torpedoes and quad AS torpedoes at the stern. Speed did not appear to be a major factor and is thought not to exceed 20 knots, while the large gaps in the dorsal surface must cause considerable underwater noise. By 1975 the missile launchers had been removed from most of this class.

After building five of these submarines the class continued with a lengthened design incorporating an additional pair of missiles. These are called Echo II or E2 by NATO, the original group being designated Echo I (E1). Rather surprisingly the E2 continued in production from 1963 until 1967 by which time twenty-seven were in operation. The additional length is only about 8 ft but it allows an extra pair of launch cylinders to be installed immediately abaft the fin. Like the E1s the bow has the latest standard suite of sonar and other sensing equipment, and the propulsion and torpedo installations remain unchanged. Echo II submarines have been seen in many parts of the world, and about a dozen are serving with both the Northern and Pacific Fleets.

Soviet Juliet class (93)
Though smaller and simpler than the Echo class these missile carriers actually ran later in timing and did

not begin to be delivered until 1962. The hull is not the same as that of any other class, and is of large beam/length ratio. It carries a very high casing to house the two pairs of Shaddock launchers, and a relatively large central fin. In the bow is the latest sonar installation, and the standard mix of large bow torpedo tubes and AS quad at the stern is fitted. Propulsion is by the standard triple diesel-electric installation. In some respects the Juliets are developments of the related F class, though functionally they succeeded Whisky Long Bin. Production continued in parallel with the much bigger nuclear Echo vessels until 1967, by which time sixteen or seventeen were in service. As in all the cruise missile submarines, the vessel must surface before launching any of its missiles and the cylinders cannot be reloaded from within the submarine. Again like all the other Shaddock carriers, there is no evidence of missile guidance equipment.

Soviet Hotel class (95)
Developed in parallel with the November class of attack submarines, the H series was the natural successor to the G class of ballistic-missile launchers, and resulted from mating the big missile-carrying fin of the G with a completely new, larger hull, propelled by nuclear power. The propulsion system is believed to be similar to that of the November, though the hull is rather more slender. Underwater speed is modest, because

these boats still do not have an optimised teardrop shape and are saddled with an extremely large fin and a noisy deck casing with a full row of free-flood perforations.

At the time of their design, in the mid-1950s, the Hotels were expected to be a major class. Production deliveries began in 1958, and as the missile system using the interim Sark (SS-N-4) was fully developed these large vessels were soon seen running on the surface in many parts of the world including areas immediately off the coast of the USA and Canada. Emergence of the Polaris system, and swift parallel development in the Soviet Union, had made the basic design obsolete by 1960 and production was held to those vessels then already started. The total was thus restricted to nine, the last being delivered in 1962. In 1963 development of the longer-range Serb (SS-N-5) missile was completed, and since then the Hotel boats have been progressively rearmed with the later weapon. Nevertheless, by today's standards it is not cost/effective to deploy such a costly launch platform for three Serb missiles. As the Strategic Arms Limitation Treaty (SALT) discussions lead to enforced reduction in the number of nuclear missile launchers in Soviet service these boats would be among the first to go. If any are retained for a long period it is likely they would be cut in two and fitted with a new section containing SS-N-6 tubes in place of the triple Serb tubes in the giant fin.

Soviet Victor class

Before the end of 1960 the Soviet Union had established in production a fully developed submarine nuclear propulsion system of standard design. At first every available reactor, heat-exchanger and turbine was needed for N, E and H class vessels, but by 1965 a design had been prepared for a completely new 'second generation' attack submarine in which the available power was used to much better effect in achieving the highest possible speed. For the first time in a Soviet submarine the hull was made of teardrop form, with diameter slightly greater than that of the November but length almost 80 ft shorter, and with great attention paid to reducing underwater drag. The fin is small and streamlined, and unlike most previous Soviet boats the bow is a bluff circular section.

All armament is concentrated in the eight 533 mm tubes in the bows. Combined with advanced sensing systems, new designs of optical periscope, improved radar and the excellent all-round performance, the V class are formidable attack submarines. On the other hand the teardrop shape is compromised by a superimposed flat-top deck casing, with many free-flood holes, which causes drag and underwater noise that is absent in the corresponding US attack submarines. Production of Victors has not been faster than about two per year, with delivery beginning in 1967, so it is doubtful that more than twenty will be in use before 1977.

Soviet Charlie class

Though completely logical in concept, these missile-firing vessels pose an even bigger problem than do the Shaddock launchers, because the weapon they carry is virtually unknown in the West. Called SS-N-7, for want of a better name, it has been described as 'similar to the Styx', but this is most unlikely. Styx (SS-N-2) is a cruise missile resembling a small aeroplane which, though boosted and then sustained by rocket thrust, flies at subsonic speed and homes on to clearly distinguished targets within a range of a little less than 30 miles. It is an obsolescent weapon, extremely bulky and easily intercepted by modern defence systems such as Seawolf. SS-N-7 must be a slender supersonic missile of totally different form, possibly sustained by body lift (or, at the most, by extremely small flick-out hinged wings), with a range at supersonic speed of about twenty-six miles. In these new submarines eight launch tubes are accommodated in a single 4×2 launcher fitted into the deck casing above the forward part of the hull. This is a most compact system, compared with either Styx or Shaddock, and a further great improvement is that any or all of the missiles can be fired at periscope depth.

Hull design is a direct linear stretch of the V class, with the same propulsion and same battery of bow torpedo tubes. The fin is substantially larger, though still low and streamlined, and it is probable that missile guidance and sensing/countermeasure systems are very extensive. As in the Victors, the pressure hull is overlain by a large flat-topped deck casing, which still requires free-flood holes though these are fewer in number than in earlier Soviet boats and apparently of a new noise-reducing design. First deliveries, said to be all from the Gorkiy yard, took place in 1968. Since then production has not exceeded three per year, and in 1975 about fifteen were in service. Their main mission appears to be to destroy hostile surface forces, for which they are extremely well equipped.

Soviet Yankee class (96)
How swiftly the Soviet Navy would have created a submarine of this calibre on its own is hard to tell. Certainly the G and H classes, with their three ballistic-missile launch tubes in a large fin, were self-evidently only stepping stones ' to a larger vessel containing multiple tubes inside a fat teardrop hull, but the Y class were inspired wholly by the US Navy FBMS and start of the Polaris build programme in 1957. Unlike the pioneer George Washington, the Y class were not a stretch of an existing hull design but a completely new design, far bigger than anything previously attempted in Europe. Indeed, because of the size of the missile, which is called Sawfly (SS-N-6) by NATO, these vessels are even bigger than their US Navy counterparts, though hydrodynamically and in most other respects they copy the American design very closely.

Fabricated from factory-built sections of nearly 35 ft diameter, the hull is cleaner than in previous Soviet submarines, and at last abandons a separate deck casing. As a result these are by far the quietest of all Soviet submarines when running underwater, and there is evidence that the propulsion system has also been quietened by the adoption of new reduction gears and careful attention to pumps. As far as is known, pumps are still used to circulate the primary coolant through the reactor closed-loop circuit, though noise signature is judged better than in the earlier vessels using the same basic propulsion system. The fin is very similar to that of the US Navy missile submarines, and carries the diving planes which in every previous Soviet production class had been on the front hull.

From the outset the Soviet government took the view that the modern FBMS-type submarine was not just important but likely to be the most important future weapon in the strategic power game. While production of other submarine classes was modest, enormous efforts have been put into first the Y class and subsequently the D class (described later) to achieve parity or dominance over the immensely formidable programme of the US Navy. Using by far the major part of the production capacity of Soviet submarine yards, with assembly of standard prefabricated sections at the highest possible rate, these huge ships have been commissioned at a rate which in 1971 reached eight per year. First delivery took place in 1967, and this Yankee prototype was subsequently at sea on extended trials in the course of which live missiles were fired in the Pacific. Four were delivered in the subsequent year, and by 1975 the total (including D class) had passed forty-two vessels, thus in terms of numbers overtaking the US Navy. Future deliveries will obviously be affected by SALT restrictions of May 1972, as discussed under the Delta heading.

Naturally these vessels can fire their missiles whilst submerged. The Sawfly missile (p.96) is significantly larger than the Polaris series, but has a comparable range and follows exactly similar technology. Unlike the earlier Serb there is no inbuilt expulsion system, and it is probable that each missile is fired out of its tube either by gas from a solid-fuel gas-generator or by steam from the propulsion system. Compared with Polaris/ Poseidon ships, these submarines are less tightly packaged, the huge hull having only a modest projecting fairing over the sixteen launch tubes. Guidance for Sawfly is conjectured to be inertial, and an inertial navigation system, with astro updating, is almost certainly fitted to the Y class submarines also. All examples appear to have a large white belt around the brow of the hull, even larger than that of the N class, suggesting an extensive series of sonar and other sensing installations. Lower down are the eight 533 mm torpedo tubes, with multi-

reload capability. The quad-400 mm AS installation is absent, possibly because of the slender stern of these hulls. No anti-aircraft armament has yet been seen on Yankees, though this may be expected eventually to be fitted. Total production appears to have been thirty-two, all delivered by the end of 1972.

Soviet Delta class

With technology as new and far-reaching as the submarine-launched ballistic missile it was hardly to be expected that the ultimate would be reached immediately. In the Soviet Union development has proceeded in more steps, over a longer period, than in the United States. Though the Sawfly missile represented a great advance over Serb, it still could not cover the whole of the continental United States, and long before the Y class vessels were being delivered work was in hand on a longer-range missile to close the gap. In the US Navy the longer-range missile turned out to be, first, successive marks of Polaris and then the Poseidon. Though the latter was substantially fatter, it was designed to be accommodated in existing launch tubes without major ship modification. In the Soviet Union such an achievement appears never to have been attempted. The fourth-generation missile to supplement Sawfly was judged too challenging a requirement to be met within anything like the same rocket vehicle dimensions, and though little is yet known about it the SS-N-8 (as it is called in the

West) is certainly considerably longer and fatter than N-6.

This meant a new class of submarine, and this has the NATO code-name of Delta, or D class. It is essentially still a Yankee, but with a considerably more prominent missile compartment projecting well above the hull profile aft of the fin. More significant is the fact that the number of launch tubes has been reduced from eight pairs to six pairs, twelve in all, suggesting that there were problems in splicing in an additional length of hull to accommodate the original number. Under the terms of the 1972 SALT agreement between Messrs Nixon and Brezhnev the Soviet Union may deploy, at any one time, up to sixty-two nuclear-powered missile submarines carrying up to 950 missiles ready to fire. This is an average of a little over fifteen missiles per submarine. Accepting that, before long, all the Golf, Hotel and (if they have nuclear warheads) Echo, Juliet and Charlie classes will be withdrawn, this means that most of the Soviet force will have to be shorter-range Yankees, each with sixteen missiles, if the maximum missile deployment is to be secured. Alternatively, a still larger submarine may be produced able to fire sixteen of the N-8 missiles.

In 1975 about ten Deltas were thought to be in service, making a total truly first-line force of forty-two submarines with 632 missiles. Of these 120 were N-8s, able to carry a sizeable thermonuclear warhead (a single warhead, it is believed) right across North America with plenty of range to spare. This missile is considered much more powerful, in terms of payload/range, than any equivalent Western missile except the new Trident. Present indications are that only Deltas are being built, the greatly increased payload and global coverage of the big missile being judged ample recompense for the slightly reduced number on board each submarine. What is on the Soviet drawing-boards?

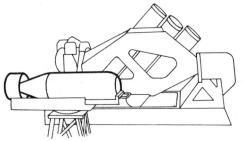

Above
A the British Squid three-barrel mortar, with bomb.
Right
B the Soviet six-barrel rocket launcher (other launchers have up to twelve barrels).

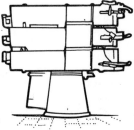

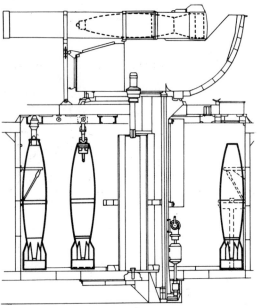

Left
C the Swedish Bofors twin-tube launcher, showing below-deck auto-loading for two 375 mm rockets each 20 seconds.

(continued)

(continued)

Left
D the Norwegian Terne Mk 8 and *right* another Swedish 375 mm rocket.

More sophisticated A/S weapons for surface ships:

Below
A French Malafon, pilotless aircraft delivering an L4 acoustic homing torpedo over ranges from 660 to 40,000 feet (200–12,000 metres).

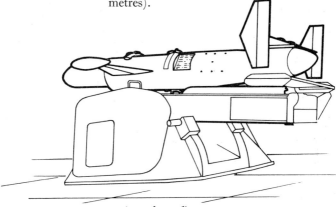

(continued)

Left

B US RUR-5A Asroc (anti-submarine rocket) fired from eight-round box or from Terrier anti-aircraft launcher over ranges to 33,000 feet (10 km), with double this range in prospect.

Below

C operation of Australian/UK Ikara system, using a guided missile to deliver a Mk 44 torpedo out to the limiting range of the ship's sonar.

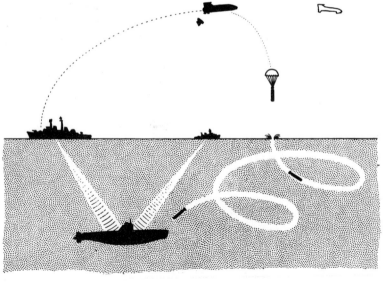

Some submarine weapons:

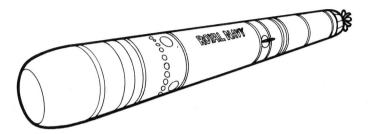

Above
A Tigerfish, the Marconi-designed torpedo which has ended more than 50 years of almost total failure in British torpedo design.

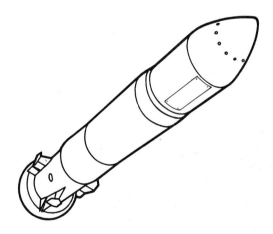

Above
B US UUM-44A Subroc, the most formidable of submarine-launched A/S weapons comprising an inertially guided rocket capable of accurately delivering a nuclear depth charge over 25–30 miles.

Some airborne A/S systems:

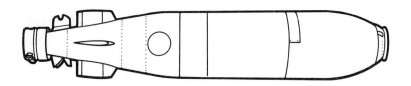

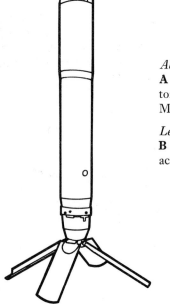

Above
A French Alcatel L4 light acoustic torpedo carried by aircraft and the Malafon missile.

Left
B French CIT air-drop passive or active sonobuoy.

(continued)

(continued)

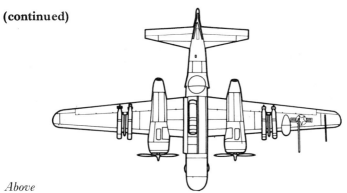

Above

C Grumman S-2D Tracker fixed-wing carrier-based aircraft, carrying radar under rear fuselage, MAD boom behind tail, 60 echo-sounding depth charges in right weapon bay, 32 sonobuoys in rear of engine nacelles, four float lights, two 5-inch rockets, four Mk 46 torpedoes and Mk 57 or 101 nuclear depth charge (seen in left weapon bay).

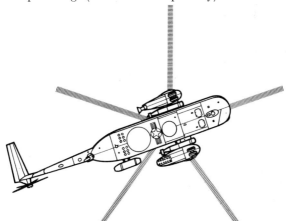

Above

D Sikorsky SH-3H Sea King ship-based helicopter, carrying radar (large ring), sonar (smaller ring), ESM (both sides of nose and under tail boom) sonobuoy launchers (12 small rings), chaff dispenser in side pod, marine marker launchers in left sponson, MAD sensor extended from right sponson, and two Mk 46 torpedoes.

	First launch	Displacement surface/ submerged (long tons)	Dimensions length/beam (feet)	Complement (officers and men)	Surface propulsion and speed (kt)	Underwater propulsion and speed (kt)
Great Britain						
Hollands	1901	104/150	63·3/11·75	1+6	250 h.p. petrol, 8·5	74 h.p. electric, 5
A class (1)	1903	165/180	100/11·5	1+10	450 h.p. petrol, 11·5	80 h.p. electric, 7
A class (2)	1904	180/207	99/12·75	2+12	550 h.p. petrol, 12	150 h.p. electric, 8
B class	1904	280/313	135/13·5	2+14	600 h.p. petrol, 13	190 h.p. electric, 8
C class	1906	290/320	143/13·5	2+14	600 h.p. petrol, 14	200 h.p. electric, 9
D1	1910	550/595	162/20·5	2+23	two 600 h.p. diesels, 16	550 h.p. electric, 9
D class	1910	560/620	165/20·5	2+23	two 875 h.p. diesels, 16	550 h.p. electric, 10
E class	1912	660/800	181/22·5	2+28	two 800 h.p. diesels, 16	840 h.p. electric, 10
G class	1915	700/975	187/22·7	2+29	two 800 h.p. diesels, 14·5	840 h.p. electric, 10
H1 class	1915	364/434	150·25/15·75	2+20	two 240 h.p. diesels, 13	320 h.p. electric, 10
H21 class	1918	440/500	171/15·75	2+20	two 240 h.p. diesels, 13	320 h.p. electric, 10
J class	1916	1,210/1,820	275·5/23	3+41	three 1,200 h.p. diesels, 19·5	1,400 h.p. electric, 9·5
K class	1916	1,883/2,565	338/26·7	3+55	two 5,250 h.p. steam turbines, 25	1,400 h.p. electric, 9
K 26	1923	2,140/2,770	351·5/28	3+62	two 5,000 h.p. steam turbines, 23·5	1,400 h.p. electric, 9
X1	1923	2,780/3,600	363·5/29·75	8+102	two 6,000 h.p. diesels, 19·5	2,600 h.p. electric, 9
M class	1918	1,600/1,950	305/24·5	60-70	two 1,200 h.p. diesels, 15·5	1,600 h.p. electric, 9·5
L1 class	1917	890/1,070	231/23·5	3+33	two 1,200 h.p. diesels, 17·5	1,600 h.p. electric, 10·5
L9 class	1917	895/1,080	238 5/23 5	3+33	two 1,200 h.p. diesels, 17·5	1,600 h.p. electric, 10·5
L50 class	1918	960/1,150	235/24	3+37	two 1,200 h.p. diesels, 17·5	1,600 h.p. electric, 10·5
R class	1917	420/500	163/15·75	2+20	one 240 h.p. diesel, 9·5	1,200 h.p. electric, 15
O class	1926	1,349/1,872	283·5/27·75	4+46	two 2,200 h.p. diesels, 17·5	1,320 h.p. electric, 9
P, R class	1929	1,475/2,040	292·5/29·75	4+46	two 2,200 h.p. diesels, 17	1,320 h.p. electric, 9
River class	1932	1,850/2,723	345/28	5+55	two 5,000 h.p. diesels, 22	2,500 h.p. electric, 10
Porpoise class	1932	1,520/2,157	293/25·5	5+50	two 1,650 h.p. diesels, 17	1,630 h.p. electric, 8·75
S class	1932	670/960	202·5/24	4+36	two 775 h.p. diesels, 13·8	1,300 h.p. electric, 10
U class (1)	1937	540/730	191·5/16	3+28	two 307·5 h.p. diesels, 11·75	825 h.p. electric, 9
U class (2)	1940	545/735	196·75/16	3+28	two 307·5 h.p. diesels, 11·2	825 h.p. electric, 9
V class	1943	545/740	206/16	4+33	two 400 h.p. diesels, 13	760 h.p. electric, 9
T class (1)	1937	1,095/1,573	275/26·5	5+54	two 1,250 h.p. diesels, 15·2	1,450 h.p. electric, 8·75
T class (2)	1951	1,535/1,740	293·5/26·5	6+59	two 1,250 h.p. diesels, 16	2,900 h.p. electric, 15
X class	1942	27/30	51·25/5·75	4	42 h.p. diesel, 6·5	30 h.p. electric, 5·5
XE class	1943	30·25/33·5	53·25/5·75	4-5	42 h.p. diesel, 6·5	30 h.p. electric, 5·5
Chariot	1942	1	21/1·7	2	electric, 2·9	—
A class (1)	1944	1,120/1,620	281·75/22·25	5+55	two 2,150 h.p. diesels, 18	1,250 h.p. electric, 8
A class (2)	1955	1,385/1,620	283/22·25	6+57	two 2,150 h.p. diesels, 19	1,250 h.p. electric, 10
Explorer	1955	780/1,120	225·5/15·7	6+44	diesel-electric	HTP steam turbine, 27
Porpoise	1956	2,030/2,405	295·25/26·5	6+65	two 1,650 h.p. diesel-electric, 12	5,000 h.p. electric, 17
Oberon	1959	2,030/2,410	295·25/26·5	7+62	two 1,840 h.p. diesel-electric, 12	6,000 h.p. electric, 17
Dreadnought	1960	3,500/4,000	265·75/32·25	11+77	S5W PWR, 15,000 h.p. 30	
Valiant	1963	3,500/4,500	285/33·2	13+90	NR2 PWR geared turbine, 30	
Swiftsure	1971	3,500/4,500	272/33·2	11+88	PWR geared turbine, 30+	
Resolution	1966	7,500/8,400	425/33	13+128	PWR geared turbine, 25	

mament (A, anti-aircraft; M, mines; T, torpedoes; TT, torpedo tubes)	No. built	Remarks
e 14 in. (bow)	5	No. 1 slightly smaller and slower
o 18 in. (bow)	4	first batch
o 18 in. (bow)	9	last (A 13) had heavy oil engine
o 18 in. (bow)	11	
o 18 in. (bow)	38	C19-38 slightly larger and faster
ree 18 in. (2 bow, 1 stern); machine-gun	1	first to have saddle tanks, diesels
ree 18 in. (2 bow, 1 stern); two 12-pdr guns	7	
e 18 in. (2 bow, 2 beam, 1 stern); one 12-pdr	57	six carried mines instead of beam tubes
ur 18 in. (2 bow, 2 beam), one 21 in. stern; one 3 in. AA	14	
ur 18 in. (bow); optional machine-gun	20	plus eight for Italy
ur 21 in. (bow, 6T); machine-gun	24	
x 18 in. (4 bow, 2 beam); 1-2×3 in. or 4 in.	7	large ocean-going boats
ght 18 in. (4 bow, 4 beam); 1-2×4 in., 1×3 in.	17	originally rearranged guns and 2TT above
n 21 in. (4 bow, 4 beam, 2 stern); three 4 in.	1	
x 21 in. (bow); 2×2 5·2 in., 4 machine-guns	1	
ur 18 in. (bow); one 12 in. gun	3	gun exchanged for seaplane (M2), mines (M3)
x 18 in. (4 bow, 2 beam); one 3 in. or 4 in.	8	
ur 21 in. (bow); two 18 in. (beam); one 4 in.	19	five carried 16 mines, in two in lieu of beam TT
x 21 in. (bow, 8T); two 4 in.	7	long superstructure
x 18 in. (bow); one 4 in.	10	AS boats, fast underwater
ght 21 in. (6 bow, 2 stern, 16T); one 4 in.	9	three differing sub-types
ght 21 in. (6 bow, 2 stern, 16T); one 4 in.	10	
x 21 in. (bow, 12T); one 4 in.	3	cost (Clyde) £459,886
x 21 in. (bow, 12T); 50 M; one 4 in.	6	cost (Rorqual) £350,639
x 21 in. (bow, 12T); one 3 in., later 20 mm AA	62	cost £230,000-245,000; some with stern tube
x (or four) 21 in. (bow, 10T); one 3 in.	15	cost £205,000 (average)
ur 21 in. (bow, 8T); one 3 in.	34	as built; modified later
ur 21 in. (bow, 8T); one 3 in.	22	
n 21 in. (8 bow, 2 deck, firing forward, later astern, 16T); one 4 in. Wartime batches, eleven TT.	53	data for first batch
x 21 in. (4 bow, 2 stern, 17T); no gun	8	as converted
o 4,400 lb charge	14	
o 4,400 lb charges	5	
0 lb warhead (Mk II, 1,100 lb)		
n 21 in. (6 bow, 4 stern, 20T); one 4 in., one 20 mm	18	can carry 26M in lieu of T
x 21 in. (4 bow, 2 stern, 16T); no gun	14	as converted
ne	2	
ght 21 in. (6 bow, 2 stern, 30T)	8	
ght 21 in. (6 bow, 20T; 2 stern, 4T)	13	
x 21 in. (bow)	1	
x 21 in. (bow)	5	
e 21 in. (bow)	4	
x 21 in. (bow); 16 Polaris A-3 tubes	4	

	First launch	Displacement surface/ submerged (long tons)	Dimensions length/beam (feet)	Complement (officers and men)	Surface propulsion and speed (kt)	Underwater propulsion and speed (kt)
United States						
Turtle	1776	2	6/4·5	1	hand-cranked screw	as for surface
Nautilus	1801	19	21·3/7	3	hand-cranked screw	as for surface
Hunley	1863	19	33/5·2	9	8-man-cranked screw	as for surface
Holland	1898	75/85	53·9/10·25	1+5	50 h.p. Otto petrol, 7	40 h.p. electric, 5·5
Protector	1902	136/174·3	67·5/14·2	7	two 120 h.p. petrol, 10	110 h.p. electric, 6·5
N class	1916	380/480	155/14·5	20	two 450 h.p. diesels, 14	200 h.p. electric, 8
O class	1918	521/629	172·25/18	3+29	two 440 h.p. diesels, 14	740 h.p. electric, 10·5
R class	1918	569/680	186·25/18	3+30	two 600 h.p. diesels, 13·5	934 h.p. electric, 10·5
S1 class	1918	854/1,062	219·25/20·75	3+39	two 600 h.p. diesels, 14·5	1,500 h.p. electric,11
S11 class	1919	876/1,092	231/21·75	3+39	two 1,000 h.p. diesels, 15	1,200 h.p. electric, 11
S42 class	1923	906/1,126	225·25/20·75	3+39	two 600 h.p. diesels, 14·5	1,500 h.p. electric, 11
Barracuda	1924	2,000/2,620	341·5/27·5	5+75	2×2 diesels, 6,700 h.p., 18	2,400 h.p. electric, 8
Argonaut	1927	2.710/4,164	381/33·75	6+83	2×2 diesels, 3,175 h.p., 15	2,400 h.p. electric, 8
Narwhal	1929	2,730/4,050	371/33·25	6+84	2×2 diesels, 5,400 h.p., 17	2,540 h.p. electric, 8
Cuttlefish	1933	1,130/1,650	274/24·75	4+46	2×2 diesels, 3,100 h.p., 17	1,600 h.p. electric, 8
Porpoise	1935	1,310/1,960	301/25	4+49	2×2 diesels, 4,300 h.p., 19	2,085 h.p. electric, 8
Salmon	1937	1,449/2,198	308/26 25	5+65	2×2 diesels, 5,500 h.p., 21	3,300 h.p. electric, 9
Sargo	1938	1,450/2,350	310·5/27	5+65	2×2 diesels, 5,500 h.p., 20	2,740 h.p. electric, 8·75
Tambor/Gar	1939	1,475/2,370	307·75/27·25	5+80	2×2 diesels, 5,400 h.p., 20	2,740 h.p. electric, 8·75
Gato	1941	1,526/2,424	311·75/27·25	5+80	2×2 diesels, 5,400 h.p., 20·25	2,740 h.p. electric, 8·75
Balao	1942	1,526/2,424	311·75/27·25	5+80	2×2 diesels, 5,400 h.p., 20·25	2,740 h.p. electric, 8·75
Tench	1944	1,570/2,428	311·75/27·25	5+85	2×2 diesels, 5,400 h.p., 20·25	2,740 h.p. electric, 8·75
Guppy III type	1960	1,975/2,450	326·5/27	85	four 1,600 h.p. diesels, 20	5,400 h.p. electric, 15
Albacore	1953	1,500/1,850	210·5/27·5	5+47	two radial pancake diesels, 25	15,000 h.p. electric, 33
Tang	1951	2,100/2,700	287/27·3	8+75	three 1,500 h.p. diesels, 16	5,600 h.p. electric, 16
Darter	1954	1,720/2,388	268·6/27·2	8+75	three 1,500 h.p. diesels, 19·5	4,500 h.p. electric, 14
Sailfish	1955	2,625/3,168	350·4/28·4	12+83	four 1,500 h.p. diesels, 19·5	8,200 h.p. electric, 14
Grayback	1957	2,670/3,650	334/30	7+60	three 1,500 h.p. diesels, 20	5,600 h.p. electric, 17
Nautilus	1954	3,530/4,040	323·7/27·6	10+95	S2W PWR reactor, two 7,500 h.p. turbines	
Barbel	1958	2,145/2,895	219·5/29	10+69	three 1,600 h.p. diesels, 15	3,150 h.p. electric, 25
Skate	1957	2,570/2,861	267·7/25	88+7	PWR, two 3,300 h.p. steam turbines, 20+	
Triton	1958	5,940/7,780	447·5/37	16+156	two S4G PWR, two 17,000 h.p. turbines, 20	
Halibut	1959	3,850/5,000	350/29·5	9+88	S3W PWR, two 3,000 h.p. turbines, 15+	
Skipjack	1958	3,075/3,500	251·7/31·5	8+85	S5W PWR, 15,000 h.p. turbine, 30+	
Tullibee	1960	2,317/2,640	273/23·3	6+56	PWR, 2,500 h.p. steam turbo-electric, 15+	
Permit	1961	3,750/4,300	278·5/31·7	12+95	S5W PWR, 15,000 h.p. turbine, 30	
Sturgeon	1966	3,860/4,630	292·2/31·7	12+95	S5W PWR, 15,000 h.p. turbine, 30	
G. Washington	1959	5,900/6,700	381·7/33	12+100	S5W PWR, 15,000 h.p. turbine, 30	
E Allen	1960	6,900/7,900	410·5/33	12+100	S5W PWR, 15,000 h.p. turbine, 30	
Lafayette	1962	7,320/8,250	425/33	14+126	S5W PWR, 15,000 h.p. turbine, 30	
Trident I	1977	/15,000	500/38	150?	PWR, 30,000+ h.p. turbine, 30	
Los Angeles	1973	5,900/6,900	360/33	12+100	PWR, 30,000 h.p. turbine, about 40	

'mament (A, anti-aircraft; M, mines; T, torpedoes; TT, torpedo tubes)	No. built	Remarks
0 lb detachable explosive charge	1	
tachable explosive charge	1	
ar torpedo, 134 lb charge	1	
e 18 in. (bow, 3T); one pneumatic 'dynamite gun' (bow)	1	many improved models followed
ree 18 in. (5T)	1	four improved models for Russia
ur 18 in. (bow); one 3 in.	7	Lakes (4) or Hollands (3)
ur 18 in. (bow); one 0·5 in. AA	10	coastal defence type
ur 21 in. (bow, 8T); one 3 in.	27	
ur 21 in. (bow, 12T); one 4 in.	33	
ur 21 in. (bow, 12T); one 4 in.	7	S11-13 one extra TT at stern
ur 21 in. (bow, 12T); one 4 in.	6	also S48, larger, five tubes
x 21 in. (4 bow, 2 stern, 12T); one 5 in.	3	gun in Bass only 3 in.
ur 21 in. (bow, 16T); two 6 in. 60M	1	long-range minelayer
x 21 in. (4 bow, 2 stern, 24T); two 6 in.	2	
x 21 in. (4 bow, 2 stern, 16T); one 3 in.	2	Cachalot fractionally smaller
x 21 in. (4 bow, 2 stern, 16T); one 4 in.	10	some 18T; various AA added
ght 21 in. (4 bow, 4 stern, 24T); one 4 in.	6	AA added later
ght 21 in. (4 bow, 4 stern, 24T); one 4 in.	10	AA added later
n 21 in. (6 bow, 4 stern, 24T); one 3 in.	12	AA added later
n 21 in. (6 bow, 4 stern, 24T); one 3 in.	73	AA added later
n 21 in. (6 bow, 4 stern, 24T); one 5 in.	122	some 4 in. gun; AA added later
n 21 in. (6 bow, 4 stern, 24T); one 5 in.	33	plus heavy AA
n 21 in. (6 bow, 4 stern)	9	last Guppy conversions of old boats
one	1	high-speed research vessel
ght 21 in. (6 bow, 2 stern)	6	first post-war design
ght 21 in. (6 bow, 2 stern)	1	last non-nuclear design
x 21 in. (bow)	2	largest US since 1930
ght 21 in. (6 bow, 2 stern)	1	transport (former missile launch)
x 21 in. (bow)	1	first nuclear submarine
x 21 in. (bow)	3	first of new spindle hull form
ght 21 in. (6 bow, 2 short tubes stern)	4	first nuclear for operations
x 21 in. (4 bow, 2 stern)	1	radar picket converted to attack
x 21 in. (4 bow, 2 stern)	1	missile launcher converted to research
x 21 in. (bow)	5	nuclear plus spindle hull
ur 21 in. (amidships)	1	quiet AS boat, whole-bow sonar
ur 21 in. (amidships) with Subroc	13	several longer and heavier
ur 21 in. (amidships) with Subroc	37	larger than Permit, taller sail
xteen Polaris A-3 tubes; six 21 in. TT (bow)	5	first SSBN (conversions)
xteen Polaris A-3 tubes; four 21 in. TT (bow)	5	
xteen Poseidon (or Polaris) tubes; four 21 in. TT (bow)	31	converting to fire Poseidon
wenty-four Trident I tubes; some TT	?	
ur 21 in. (amidships) with Subroc	18	

	First launch	Displacement surface/ submerged (long tons)	Dimensions length/beam (feet)	Complement (officers and men)	Surface propulsion and speed (kt)	Underwater propulsion and speed (kt)
Russia and Soviet Union						
Akula	1910	370/468	187/12	20	three 300 h.p. diesels, 10·5	300 h.p. electric, 6·5
L class	1929	896/1,318	279/23	5+39	two 1,250 h.p. diesels, 15	1,200 h.p. electric, 8
Chuka (Shch)	1933	650/740	190·25/19·5	5+35	two 800 h.p. diesels, 15	800 h.p. electric, 9
M IV	1946	350/420	167/16	3+21	two 500 h.p. diesels, 13	800 h.p. electric, 11
W class	1952	1,030/1,350	240/22	5+55	two 2,000 h.p. diesels, 17	2,500 h.p. electric, 15
W twin-cylinder	1958	1,100/1,450	240/22	60+	two 2,000 h.p. diesels, 17	2,500 h.p. electric, 13
W long bin	1959	1,350/1,800	270·6/22	60+	two 2,000 h.p. diesels, 17	2,500 h.p. electric, 13
Zulu	1954	1,950/2,200	295·3/23·9	6+64	two 5,000 h.p. diesels, 18	3,500 h.p. electric, 16
Foxtrot	1956	1,960/2,300	299/26	6+64	two 5,000 h.p. diesels, 18	4,000 h.p. electric, 17
Quebec	1958	560/740	184/18	5+35	two 1,500 h.p. diesels, 18	2,500 h.p. electric, 16
Romeo	1958	1,100/1,600	256/24	5+60	two 2,000 h.p. diesels, 18·5	3,500 h.p. electric, 15
Golf II	1959	2,350/2,800	328/25	12+74	three 2,000 h.p. diesels, 17·6	6,000 h.p. electric, 17
November	1961	3,500/4,000	361/32·1	10+78	PWR geared turbine, 20 surf., 25	
Echo II	1961	5,000/5,600	387·4/28·4	14+88	PWR turbine, 22,500 h.p., 20	
Juliet	1962	2,200/2,500	281/31·4	8+62	two 3,000 h.p. diesels, 16	6,000 h.p. electric, 16
Hotel	1959	3,700/4,100	377/28·2	12+78	PWR turbine, 22,500 h.p., 20	
Victor	1965	3,600/4,200	285/33	90?	PWR geared turbine, 26 surf., 30+	
Charlie	1966	4,300/5,100	295/32·8	10+90	PWR turbine, 24,000 h.p., 30	
Yankee	1966	8,000/9,000	427/34·8	15+105	PWR turbine, 24,000 h.p., 25	
Delta	1973	8,100/9,980	427/	120?	PWR turbine, 24,000 h.p., 25	
Germany						
Brandtaucher	1850	38·5	26·5/8	3	treadmill screw	as for surface
Karp (UI)	1905	238/283	139/12·25	1+18	two 200 h.p. heavy oil, 10·7	400 h.p. electric, 7
Desiderata (U5)	1910	505/636	188/18·25	2+26	two 450 h.p. heavy oil, 13·5	1,040 h.p. electric, 10
Mittel U	1913	650/837	210·5/20	2+37	two 850 h.p. diesels, 15·5	1,200 h.p. electric, 9·5
UB I	1915	127/142	92·25/9·75	1+13	60 h.p. heavy oil, 6·5	120 h.p. electric, 5·5
UB II	1915	263/292	118·5/14·5	2+21	two 142 h.p. diesels, 9	280 h.p. electric, 5·75
UB III	1917	520/650	182/19	2+32	two 550 h.p. diesels, 13·5	788 h.p. electric, 7·5
UC I	1915	168/183	111·5/10·3	1+14	90 h.p. heavy oil, 6·5	175 h.p. electric, 5·25
UC II	1916	434/511	173/17	2+24	two 300 h.p. diesels, 12	620 h.p. electric, 7·4
UC III	1918	491/571	185·3/18·25	2+30	two 300 h.p. diesels, 11·5	770 h.p. electric, 6·6
UE I	1915	755/830	186·3/19·3	2+37	two 450 h.p. diesels, 10	900 h.p. electric, 7·9
UE II	1918	1,164/1,512	267·5/24·3	2+38	two 1,200 h.p. diesels, 14·75	1,240 h.p. electric, 7·25
UA	1918	1,930/2,483	311/29·75	62-83	two 1,750 h.p. diesels, 16	1,780 h.p. electric, 8
Type IA	1936	862/1,200	237/20·3	4+39	two 1,500 h.p. diesels, 17·8	1,000 h.p. electric, 8
Type IIA	1935	254/380	134/13·4	3+22	two 350 h.p. diesels, 13	360 h.p. electric, 6·9
Type IIB	1935	279/414	140/13·4	3+22	two 350 h.p. diesels, 12·5	360 h.p. electric, 7
Type IIC	1938	291/435	144/13·4	3+22	two 350 h.p. diesels, 12	410 h.p. electric, 7
Type IID	1940	314/460	144·4/16	3+22	two 350 h.p. diesels, 12·7	410 h.p. electric, 7·4
Type VIIA	1936	626/915	211·6/19·4	4+40	two 1,150 h.p. diesels, 16	750 h.p. electric, 8
Type VIIC	1940	769/1,070	218/20·3	44-56	two 1,400 h.p. diesels, 17	750 h.p. electric, 8
Type VIID	1941	965/1,285	251/21	4+40	two 1,600 h.p. diesels, 17	750 h.p. electric, 8
Type VIIF	1943	1,084/1,345	251/24	4+42	two 1,600 h.p. diesels, 17	750 h.p. electric, 7·5
Type IXA	1938	1,032/1,408	251/21·3	4+44	two 2,200 h.p. diesels, 16	1,000 h.p. electric, 7·3

nament (A, anti-aircraft; M, mines; T, torpedoes; TT, torpedo tubes)	No. built	Remarks
...nt 18 in. (2 bow, 2 stern, 4 external cradles)	1	Baltic fleet; 2 others similar
...ht 21 in. (6 bow, 2 stern); one 4 in., one 37 mm	60?	preceded by many other small groups
...r (later 6) 21 in. (bow); 20M; two 45 mm	80+	many variants
...) 21 in. (18 in. in earlier versions); one 45 mm	200?	coastal; original design 1928
...21 in. (4 bow, 2 stern, 18T); guns removed	276	many variants
...r 21 in. (bow); two pivoted Shaddock tubes	6?	preceded by 'single-cylinder'
...r 21 in. (bow); four internal Shaddock tubes	15?	
...21 in. (6 bow, 4 stern) 24T or 10T+40M	35	also 10? Z V, missile trials
...ht (or ten) 21 in. (6 bow, 2-4 stern, 20T)	40	
...r 21 in. (bow); guns removed	15+	
...21 in. (bow)	15?	
...21 in. (bow); three N-5 Serb tubes	30	
...21 in. (bow); four 16 in. (stern)	13	
...21 in. (bow); four 16 in. (stern); eight Shaddock tubes	27	preceded by small EI (3)
...21 in. (bow); four 16 in. (stern); four Shaddock tubes	16	
...21 in. (bow); four 16 in. (stern); three N-5 Serb tubes	9	
...ght 21 in. (bow)	18?	
...ht 21 in. (bow); eight SS-N-7 launchers	11	
...ght 21 in. (bow); 16 N-6 Sawfly tubes	32	
...elve SS-N-8 tubes; eight 21 in. TT (bow)	4+	
...tachable explosive charge	1	
...e 17·7 in. (bow)	1	larger 4-tube U2-4 followed
...ur 17·7 in. (2 bow, 2 stern); one 2 in. gun	14	later batches more powerful
...ur 19·7 in. (2 bow, 2 stern); one 3·4 or 4·1 in.	97	some six 19·7 in., more power
...o 17·7 in. (bow)	17	UB9-17 faster than first 8
...ro 19·7 in. (bow); one 3·4 or 2 in.	30	UB30-47 fractionally larger
...e 19·7 in. (4 bow, 1 stern); one 3·4 or 4·1 in.	96	final 11 fractionally larger
...x M tubes, 12M	15	coastal minelayers
...ree 19·7 in. (2 bow, 1 stern); six M tubes (18M); 1×3·4 in.	64	bow tubes above water on surface
...ree 19·7 in. (2 external, firing ahead, 1 stern); six M tubes (14M); 1×3·4 in.	25	
...o 19·7 in. (deck); 21M; one 3·4 or 4·1 in.	10	short-range minelayers
...ur 19·7 in. (bow); 42-48M; 1-2×5·9 in.	10	long-range minelayers
...19·7 in. (4 bow, 2 stern); two 5·9 in.	3	four smaller U135s and big U142
...x 21 in. (4 bow, 2 stern); one 4·1 in; one 20 mm AA	2	
...ree 21 in. (bow); 2-4×20 mm AA	6	coastal
...ree 21 in. (bow); 2-4×20 mm AA	20	
...ree 21 in. (bow); 2-4×20 mm AA	8	
...ree 21 in. (bow); 2-4×20 mm AA	16	'long-range coastal'
...ve 21 in. (4 bow, 1 stern); one 3·4 in., one 20 mm	10	long range
...ve 21 in. (4 bow, 1 stern, 14T); up to 8×20 mm AA	677	or 3·4 in., or 37 mm AA
...ve 21 in. (4 bow, 1 stern); 15M; one 3·4 in. various AA	6	minelayers
...ve 21 in. (4 bow, 1 stern); one 3·4 in., one 37 mm, two 20 mm	4	21 T as cargo
...x 21 in. (4 bow, 2 stern, 22T); one 3·4 in., one 37 mm, 4×20 mm	8	ocean-going attack submarine

	First launch	Displacement surface/submerged (long tons)	Dimensions length/beam (feet)	Complement (officers and men)	Surface propulsion and speed (kt)	Underwater propulsion and speed (kt)
Type IXC	1940	1,120/1,540	250·5/22·3	4+44	two 2,200 h.p. diesels, 18·3	1,000 h.p. electric, 7·3
Type IXD	1941	1,610/2,150	287/24·6	4+51	two 1,600 h.p. diesels, 17	1,000 h.p. electric, 7
Type IXD₂	1941	1,616/2,150	287/24·6	55-65	2×2 diesels, 5,400 h.p., 19	1,000 h.p. electric, 6·9
Type XB	1941	1,763/2,710	295/30·2	5+47	two 2,400 h.p. diesels, 17	1,100 h.p. electric, 7
Type XIV	1941	1,688/2,300	220·2/30·85	6+47	two 1,600 h.p. diesels, 15	750 h.p. electric, 6·5
Type XVIIA	1943	236/280	112/11·15	2+10	210 h.p. diesel-electric, 9	5,000 h.p. Walter turbine, 26
Type XVIIB	1944	312/415	136·2/14·7	3+16	210 h.p. diesel-electric, 8·8	2,500 h.p. Walter turbine, 25
Type XXI	1944	1,621/2,100	251·5/26·25	5+52	two 2,000 h.p. diesel-electric, 15·6	5,000 h.p. electric, 16·8
Type XXIII	1944	234/275	113·1/9·85	2+12	630 h.p. diesel-electric, 9·7	580 h.p. electric, 12·5
Neger	1944	about 5	26·7/1·95	1	12 h.p. electric, 20	could not submerge
Marder	1944	about 5	26·7/1·95	1	12 h.p. electric, 19	
Biber	1944?	6.25/7	29·5/3·7	1	batteries charged 32 h.p. petrol	13 h.p. electric, 10
Molch	1944	10·5/11	35·8/4·3	1	13 h.p. electric, 5	
Type XXVIIA	1944	11·75/12·5	34·4/4·3	2	12 h.p. electric, 6	
Type XXVIIB	1944	15/16	39/5·8	2	batteries charged 60 h.p. diesel	11 h.p. electric, 6

Japan

	First launch	Displacement surface/submerged (long tons)	Dimensions length/beam (feet)	Complement (officers and men)	Surface propulsion and speed (kt)	Underwater propulsion and speed (kt)
KD1 (I 51)	1921	1,500/2,430	300/29	4+56	two 2,600 h.p. diesels, 20	2,000 h.p. electric, 10
KD2 (I 152)	1922	1,500/2,500	331/25	4+56	two 3,400 h.p. diesels, 22	2,000 h.p. electric, 10
L3 (RO 57)	1921	897/1,195	250/23·5	4+56	two 1,200 h.p. diesels, 17	1,600 h.p. electric, 8
KT (RO 29)	1922	777/998	243/20	4+56	two 600 h.p. diesels, 13	1,200 h.p. electric, 8
L4 (RO 60)	1922	996/1,320	250/24·5	4+56	two 1,200 h.p. diesels, 16	1,600 h.p. electric, 8
J1 (I 1)	1924	2,135/2,791	320/30·25	5+75	two 3,000 h.p. diesels, 18	2,600 h.p. electric, 8
KD3 (I 153)	1925	1,800/2,300	330/26	4+56	two 3,400 h.p. diesels, 20	1,800 h.p. electric, 8
KRS (I 121)	1926	1,383/1,768	281/24·5	5+70	two 1,200 h.p. diesels, 14·5	1,100 h.p. electric, 7
KD4 (I 64)	1927	1,720/2,300	320·5/25·5	4+56	two 3,000 h.p. diesels, 20	1,800 h.p. electric, 8·5
KD5 (I 165)	1931	1,705/2,330	320·5/26·75	5+70	two 3,000 h.p. diesels, 20·5	1,800 h.p. electric, 8
J1M (I 5)	1931	2,243/3,061	320/30·6	5+75	two 3,000 h.p. diesels, 18	2,600 h.p. electric, 8
KD6A (I 168)	1933	1,785/2,440	343·5/27	5+65	two 4,500 h.p. diesels, 23	1,800 h.p. electric, 8
J3 (I 7)	1935	2,525/3,583	358·5/29·75	5+95	two 5,600 h.p. diesels, 23	2,800 h.p. electric, 8
C1 (I 16)	1938	2,554/3,561	358·5/30	5+95	two 6,200 h.p. diesels, 23·5	2,000 h.p. electric, 8
BI (I 15)	1939	2,584/3,654	356·5/30·5	5+95	two 6,200 h.p. diesels, 23·5	2,000 h.p. electric, 8
KS (RO 100)	1942	601/782	200/20	5+70	two 550 h.p. diesels, 14	760 h.p. electric, 8
KD7 (RO 176)	1941	1,833/2,602	346/27	5+75	two 4,000 h.p. diesels, 23	1,800 h.p. electric, 8
K6 (RO 35)	1942	1,115/1,447	264/23	5+75	two 2,100 h.p. diesels, 19·5	1,200 h.p. electric, 8·5
C3 (I 52)	1943	2,564/3,644	356·5/30·5	5+95	two 2,350 h.p. diesels, 17	1,200 h.p. electric, 6·5
DI (I 361)	1943	1,779/2,215	241/29·25	5+70	two 925 h.p. diesels, 13	1,200 h.p. electric, 6·5
SH (I 351)	1944	3,512/4,290	364/34	6+84	two 1,850 h.p. diesels, 15·5	1,200 h.p. electric, 6
STo (I 400)	1944	5,223/6,560	400·25/39·3	6+94	two 3,750 h.p. diesels, 18·5	2,400 h.p. electric, 6·5
ST (I 201)	1944	1,291/1,450	259/19	5+95	two 1,375 h.p. diesels, 15·75	5,000 h.p. electric, 19
SS (Ha 101)	1944	429/493	146/20	2+20	400 h.p. diesel, 10	150 h.p. electric, 5
STS (Ha 201)	1945	377/440	174/13	2+20	400 h.p. diesel, 10·5	1,250 h.p. electric, 13
Midget A	1938	45/46	78·5/6	2	600 h.p. electric, 23	as for surface, 19
Midget C	1942	47/49·8	80·5/8·5	3	batteries charged 40 h.p. diesel	600 h.p. electric, 18½
D (Koryn)	1944	—/59·3	86/6·5	5	batteries charged 150 h.p. diesel	500 h.p. electric, 16
Kairyu	1944	—/19·25	55·5/4·5	2	85 h.p. petrol, 7·5	80 h.p. electric, 10
Kaiten 1	1944	—/8·3	48·3/3·2	1	550 h.p. torpedo engine, 35	
Kaiten 2	1945	—/18·3	54/4·5	2	1,500 h.p. Perhydrol turbine, 35	

Armament (AA, anti-aircraft; M, mines; T, torpedoes; TT, torpedo tubes)	No. built	Remarks
four 21 in. (4 bow, 2 stern, 22T); one 4·1 in. plus AA	138	
one at first, but multiple AA	2	long-range tanker
four 21 in. (4 bow, 2 stern, 24T); one 4·1 in. plus AA	31	fighting tanker
two 21 in. (stern); 15T, 22M or 66M; 4·1 in. plus AA	8	minelayer
no TT; 1-2×37 mm, 2-4×20 mm AA	10	Milch Cow tankers
two 21 in. (bow, 4T)	4	first closed-cycle propulsion
two 21 in. (bow, 4T)	3	
six 21 in. (bow); 23T or 12T/12M; 4×20 mm or 30 mm	125	new standard seagoing boat
two 21 in. (bow, no reloads)	64	coastal
one T underslung	200	could not submerge
one T underslung	300	diving version of Neger
two T recessed below	324	
two T carried on external racks	390	
one T or one M carried below	4	Hecht midget
two T carried on external racks	250	Seehund midget
eight 21 in. (bow, 24T); one 4·7 in.	1	remarkable for its day
eight 21 in. (bow, 16T); one 4·7 in., one 3 in.	1	
four 21 in. (bow, 10T); one 3 in.	3	
four 21 in. (bow, 8T); one 4·7 in.	4	K5 (RO 33) class of two boats similar
six 21 in. (bow, 10T); one 3 in.	9	
six 21 in. (bow, 20T); two 5·5 in.	4	range 27,600 miles at 10 kt
eight 21 in. (bow, 16T); one 4·7 in.	9	
four 21 in. (bow, 12T); 42M; one 5·5 in.	4	based on German UA
six 21 in. (bow, 14T); one 4·7 in.	3	
six 21 in. (bow, 14T); one 3·9 in.	3	
six 21 in. (bow, 20T); two 5·5 in.	1	J2 (I6) similar
six 21 in. (bow, 14T); one 3·9 or 4·7 in.	6	KD6B (I 174-5) similar
six 21 in. (bow, 20T); one 5·5 in., 2×13 mm	2	A1 (I 9-11) and A2 (I 12) similar, plus aircraft
eight 21 in. (bow, 20T); one 5·5 in., 2×25 mm	5	C2 (I 46-48) similar
six 21 in. (bow, 17T); one 5·5 in., 2×25 mm	20	seaplane; B2 (I 40-45) similar
four 21 in. (bow, 5T); one 3 in.	18	coastal
six 21 in. (bow, 12T); one 4·7 in., 2×25 mm	10	
four 21 in. (bow, 10T); one 3 in., 2×25 mm	18	63 units cancelled
six 21 in. (bow, 19T); two 5·5 in., 2×25 mm	3	B3 (I 54, 56, 58) similar plus seaplane
no TT; one 5·5 in., 2×25 mm	12	82 tons cargo, landing craft, etc; D2 (I 373) similar
four 21 in. (bow, 4T); 4×76 mm mortars, 7×25 mm	2	supply ships for marine aircraft
eight 21 in. (bow, 20T); one 5·5 in., 10×25 mm	4	three bomber aircraft
four 21 in. (bow, 10T); 2×25 mm	6	many left unfinished
no TT; one 25 mm	12	60 tons cargo
two 21 in. (bow, 4T); one 7·7 mm	10	70 scrapped or cancelled
two 18 in. (bow)	60	used at Pearl Harbor
two 18 in. (bow)	15	plus one type B
two 18 in. (bow)	115	over 400 unfinished
two 18 in., external, or 1,320 lb warhead	207	
warhead 3,418 lb	200+	
warhead 3,418 lb (later 3,968 lb)	10?	

	First launch	Displacement surface/ submerged (long tons)	Dimensions length/beam (feet)	Complement (officers and men)	Surface propulsion and speed (kt)	Underwater propulsion and speed (kt)
France						
Le Plongeur	1863	420/450	140/20	8?	compressed-air (180 lb/sq. in.) piston engine	as surface
Narval	1899	106/168	111·5/12·3	8	250 h.p. triple-expansion, 11	150 h.p. electric, 8
Brumaire	1911	400/505	172/17·75	3+23	two 420 h.p. diesels, 13	600 h.p. electric, 9
Amarante	1913	410/550	176/16·4	3+27	two 600 h.p. diesels, 14	410 h.p. electric, 8
Dupuy de Lòme	1915	833/1,100	246·7/21	4+46	two 2,000 h.p. steam turbine, 18	1,000 h.p. electric, 11
Requin	1924	974/1,441	256·7/22·4	4+50	two 1,450 h.p. diesels, 15	1,800 h.p. electric, 9
Redoutable	1928	1,570/2,084	303/26·9	4+57	two 3,000 h.p. diesels, 19	2,000 h.p. electric, 10
Surcouf	1929	3,304/4,218	361/29·5	8+110	two 3,800 h.p. diesels, 18	3,400 h.p. electric, 8·5
Circé	1925	615/776	205/17·7	3+38	two 625 h.p. diesels, 14	1,000 h.p. electric, 7·5
Sirène	1925	609/757	209·9/17·1	3+38	two 650 h.p. diesels, 13·5	1,000 h.p. electric, 7·5
Ariane	1925	626/787	216/16·3	3+38	two 600 h.p. diesels, 14	1,000 h.p. electric, 7·5
Argonaute	1929	630/798	208/17	3+38	two 650 h.p. diesels, 14	1,000 h.p. electric, 9
Diane	1930	651/807	211/17	3+38	two 650 h.p. diesels, 13·7	1,000 h.p. electric, 9·2
Orion	1931	656/822	211/17	3+38	two 710 h.p. diesels, 14	1,100 h.p. electric, 9·2
Minerve	1934	662/856	223·2/18·4	3+39	two 900 h.p. diesels, 14·3	1,230 h.p. electric, 9·3
Saphir	1928	761/925	216/23·2	3+39	two 650 h.p. diesels, 12	1,100 h.p. electric, 9
La Créole	1940	970/1,250	241/21·3	7+55	two 1,500 h.p. diesels, 17·3	1,400 h.p. electric, 10
Narval	1955	1,640/1,910	257/23·75	7+56	three 1,350 h.p. diesels (two shafts), 15	4,800 h.p. electric, 18
Aréthuse	1957	543/669	164/19	6+34	1,060 h.p. diesel, 12·5	1,300 h.p. electric, 16
Daphne	1959	869/1,043	190·25/22·25	6+39	two 650 h.p. diesels, 13	1,600 h.p. electric, 16
Le Redoutable	1967	7,500/9,000	420/34·8	12+130	PWR, 15,000 h.p. turbo-electric, nearly 30	
Agosta	1974	1,230/1,725	222/22·3	7+50	diesel-electric, 9	electric, 20
Agosta	1978	1,230/3,000	240/30	7+50	PWR, nearly 40	
Italy						
X2	1917	403/468	139/18·1	2+22	two 325 h.p. diesels, 8·2	325 h.p. electric, 6·3
Balilla	1927	1,450/1,904	284/25·6	7+70	two 2,450 h.p. diesels, 17·5	2,200 h.p. electric, 8
Mameli	1927	824/1,009	212/20	5+44	two 1,550 h.p. diesels, 17·2	1.100 h.p. electric. 7·7
E. Fieramosca	1929	1,556/2,128	276/27·2	7+71	two 2,600 h.p. diesels, 19	2,000 h.p. electric, 8
Bandiera	1929	940/1,153	229/23·7	5+47	two 1,500 h.p. diesels, 15·1	1,300 h.p. electric, 8·2
Bragadin	1929	981/1,086	234·5/20·2	6+50	two 750 h.p. diesels, 11·5	1,000 h.p. electric, 7
Argonauta	1931	660/810	202/18·7	4+40	two 600 h.p. diesels, 14	800 h.p. electric, 8
Sirena	1933	690/850	197/21·1	5+40	two 600 h.p. diesels, 14	800 h.p. electric, 8
Glauco	1935	1,071/1,326	239·5/23·6	7+52	two 1,500 h.p. diesels, 17·2	1,200 h.p. electric, 8
Calvi	1935	1,550/2,060	276/25·25	9+68	two 2,200 h.p. diesels, 17	1,800 h.p. electric, 7·5
Foca	1938	1,320/1,650	272/23·5	8+53	two 1,440 h.p. diesels, 15·8	1,250 h.p. electric, 7·7
Marcello	1938	1,063/1,317	239/23·6	7+50	two 1,800 h.p. diesels, 17·5	1,100 h.p. electric, 8·2
Cagni	1940	1,680/2,170	288·5/25·4	10+75	two 2,185 h.p. diesels, 17	1,800 h.p. electric, 9
Acciaio	1941	710/870	197/21·1	6+40	two 750 h.p. diesels, 14·5	800 h.p. electric, 7·5
Remo	1943	2,190/2,600	284/23·2	7+56	two 1,380 h.p. diesels, 14	900 h.p. electric, 6·5
CB midget	1941	36/45	49/9·8	1+3	50 h.p. diesel, 7·5	80 h.p. electric, 7
SLC torpedo	1938	1·5	22/1·8	2	1·1 or 1·6 h.p. petrol, 2·3	
Netherlands						
O 19	1938	967/1,468	264·75/23·75	3+35	two 2,650 h.p. diesels, 20	1,000 h.p. electric, 9
Dolfijn	1959	1,494/1,826	261/25·8	5+59	two 1,550 h.p. diesels, 14·5	4,200 h.p. electric, 17
Sweden						
Sjölejonet	1936	580/760	204/20·5	3+29	two 1,500 h.p. diesels, 15	1,000 h.p. electric, 10
Sjöhunden	1967	1,100/1,400	167·3/20	4+19	1,900 h.p. diesel, 15	3,500 h.p. electric, 20

rmament (AA, anti-aircraft; M, mines; T, torpedoes; TT, torpedo tubes)	No. built	Remarks
ne spar T	1	
our 17·75 in. T on external cradles	1	originally less powerful
even 17·75 in. T on external cradles; one 3-pdr	13	previously 11 similar Pluviose (steam)
ight 17·75 in. T in TT or cradles; one 3-pdr	5	
ight 17·75 in. T in TT or cradles; two 14-pdr	2	Lagrange (4) similar but 10T
en 21·7 in. (4 bow, 2 stern, 2×2 deck); one 3·9 in.	9	deck tubes in revolving mounts
ine 21·7 in. (4 bow, 3 deck, 2 deck) and two 15·75 in. (deck); one 3·9 in.	31	three sets revolving tubes
ight 21·7 in. (4 bow, 4 deck, 80T) and four 15·75 in. (deck); two 8 in., two 37 mm	1	revolving deck tubes; seaplane
even 21·7 in. (3 bow, 2 stern, 2 deck); one 75 mm	4	Schneider-Laubeuf type
even 21·7 in. (3 bow, 2 stern, 2 deck); one 75 mm	3	Loire-Simonot type
even 21·7 in. (3 bow, 2 stern, 2 deck); one 75 mm	3	Normand-Fernaux type
ix 21·7 in. (3 bow, 2+1 deck) and two 15·75 in. (deck); one 75 mm	5	Schneider-Laubeuf type
ix 21·7 in. (3 bow, 2+1 deck) and two 15·75 in. (deck); one 75 mm	9	Normand-Fenaux type
ix 21·7 in. (3 bow, 2+1 deck) and two 15·75 in. (deck); one 75 mm	2	Loire-Simonot type
x 21·7 in. (3 bow, 3 deck) and three 15·75 in. (deck); one 75 mm	6	Standard Amiranté type
hree 21·7 in. (2 bow, 1 deck); two 15·75 in. (deck); 32M; one 75 mm	6	efficient Normand-Fenaux minelayers
en 21·7 in. (6 bow, 4 deck firing aft); one 3·5 in.	4	completed 1949-53
ix 21·7 in. (bow, 20T)	6	as reconstructed
our 21 in. (bow, 20T)	4	hunter-killers
welve 21·7 in. (8 bow, 4 deck astern, 16T)	9	plus exported or licensed versions (14)
ixteen MSBS tubes; four 21·7 in. (18T)	5	largest non-Soviet submarines
our 21·7 in. (bow, 20T)	4	plus two building by Spain; four S. Africa
ot disclosed	?	first order 1975
wo 17·7 in. (bow, 2T); 9M tubes (18M); one 3 in.	2	
ix 21 in. (16T); Balilla only, 4M; one 4·7 in.	4	
six 21 in. (10T); one 4 in., two 13·2 mm AA	4	Pisani (4) similar
ight 21 in. (14T); one 4·7 in., 13·2 mm AA	1	hangar but no aircraft
ight 21 in. (12T); one 4 in., two 13·2 mm AA	4	Squalo (4), Settembrini (2), similar
our 21 in. (6T); two M tubes (16-24M); one 4 in., two 13·2 mm	2	
six 21 in. (12T); one 4 in., two 13·2 mm AA	7	
six 21 in. (12T); one 3·9 in., 2-4×13·2 mm	12	Perla (10), Adua (17), Argo (2) similar
ight 21 in. (14T); two 3·9 in., two 13·2 mm AA	2	Archimede (2 Italy, 2 Spain) similar
ight 21 in. (16T); two 4·7 in., four 13·2 mm	3	Pietro Micca (6TT, 20M) similar
six 21 in. (8T); 36M; one 3·9 in., four 13·2 mm	3	
ight 21 in. (16T); two 3·9 in., four 13·2 mm	9	Cappellini (2), Brin (5), Liuzzi (4) and Marconi (6) similar
ourteen 17·7 in. (36T); two 3·9 in. four 13·2 mm	4	small TT for commerce raiding
six 21 in. (8T); one 3·9 in., 1-2×20 mm, 2-4×13·2 mm	13	Flutto I (9) and II (none completed) similar
no TT (2×17·7 in. later); 3×20 mm AA	2	transports (610 ton load), 10 unfinished
two 17·7 in., T external, or two M	6	16 unfinished
explosive charge of 485, 551 or 661 lb	80+	
ight 21 in. (4 bow, 2 stern, 2 deck); 40M; one 3·5.	1	Polish Orzel (2) and Dolfijn, Zwaardvisch, similar
ight 21 in. (4 bow, 4 stern, 16T)	4	originally two each of two classes
six 21 in. (3 bow, 1 stern, 2 deck); two 40 mm AA	9	Delfinen (3), Najaden (3), 4TT+20M
four 21 in. (bow)	5	

INDEX

Figures in **bold** refer to plate numbers.

359.8 Gunston, Bill
GUN
        Submarines in color

WITHDRAWN

OCT 10 '78	DATE		
NOV 15 '78			
MAY 2 '79			
MAY 24 '79			
SEP 21 '79			
NOV 26 '79			

© THE BAKER & TAYLOR CO.